*By buying this book you are directly supporting
the mission of Green Card Voices.*

"Atlanta's story as a rising destination for people from across the globe has rarely been as poignantly told as through this exceptional book, celebrating the voices of its next generation. As a growing movement of local leaders work to counter divisive rhetoric and build inclusive communities, this powerful collection will not only be a resource to them, but reminds us of exactly what is at stake—and that no matter where we come from, we share the same dreams and aspirations."

—Rachel Perić, Executive Director, Welcoming America

"This book brings a face to the otherwise faceless immigration issue. It provides stories from real life that colorfully describe the challenges these brave young people have encountered. This is not a book about refugees. It is a book by refugees, young ones, passionate ones. Just as Atlanta has become an economic powerhouse, so, too, has it been a leader in the Civil Rights Movement. These stories give us the color we need to paint a picture of a greater Atlanta that practices the Biblical mandate to welcome strangers in our midst. *Green Card Youth Voices* is an invaluable resource for faith communities struggling with anti-immigrant sentiment. It should be read by every high school social studies student and by every undergraduate global studies major."

—Dr. Joseph G. Bock, Director, School of Conflict Management, Peacebuilding and Development, Kennesaw State University

"These poignant essays, written by teen immigrants, offer powerful opportunities for readers to experience empathy, understanding more clearly both the uniqueness of each person's story and the ways we all are bound together. At times heartbreaking, but also encouraging and inspiring, *Green Card Youth Voices: Immigration Stories from an Atlanta High School*, affirms how fortunate we are, in the United States, that this young generation of immigrants is building a better future for us all."

—Dr. Marie Marquardt, Author of Young Adult novels *Flight Season*, *The Radius of Us*, and *Dream Things True*

"*Green Card Youth Voices: Immigration Stories from an Atlanta High School* allows us to bear witness to the formidable strength and resilience of our country's immigrant youth. At a time when immigrant children—including those seeking protection and family reunification—face insurmountable barriers, immigrant youth voices helps us discern facts from false-rhetoric, humanity from fear-mongering. These powerful voices shed light on the journey, the struggles, and the undeniable hopes and dreams of immigrant youth. I want to thank each and every one of them for inspiring us and for allowing us to stand with them as they forge ahead during these uncertain times with great valor and determination."

—Maria M. Odom, Vice President for Legal Services, Kids in Need of Defense (KIND)

"I was moved to tears reading these stories. These are our children; their stories are our stories. Their voices crackle with hope and courage and humor and grit—they will make you laugh, they will make you cry, but most of all, they will open your eyes to see and appreciate more fully the humanity of our immigrant brothers and sisters. Thank you for this book. We need these stories."

—Andrew Haile, Assistant Attorney General, Office of the Massachusetts Attorney General and Freelance Writer for *The Washington Post*

"It is powerful to be able to capture the history of new Americans in this nation. These incredible narratives give hope to many immigrants who still find themselves questioning how they fit into the history of America. These courageous young men and women give faces and breath to the many stories of immigrants and refugees who have immigrated, been resettled, or will be arrive in the United States. *Green Card Youth Voices* is game-changing."

—Victoria Huynh, Vice President, Center for Pan Asian Community Services, Inc.

"The future growth and development of Atlanta and communities across the South is inextricably linked to immigrants. But in the current toxic political environment our understanding of their stories and hopes are drowned out. *Green Card Youth Voices* presents an honest and informed account of young immigrants' lives; their struggles, hopes, and aspirations. Community leaders from business, faith communities, and government need to read this powerful collection of stories. It will broaden understanding and help inform future community decisions that will make Atlanta and our region a stronger and better place for everyone."
— **Dr. Owen J. Furuseth, Associate Provost for Metropolitan Studies and Extended Academic Programs and Professor Emeritus, University of North Carolina at Charlotte**

"For nearly half a century, the Latin American Association has worked to empower Georgia Latino youth to share their stories with the world and to create positive change in their communities. *Green Card Youth Voices* elevates the experiences of Latino and immigrant youth. Their compelling narratives invite the reader into their world, highlighting stories of struggle, persistence, and triumph that represent the very best of the American spirit."
— **Anibal Torres, Executive Director, The Latin American Association**

"*Green Card Youth Voices: Immigration Stories from an Atlanta High School* demonstrates the power of narratives and storytelling. If the goal is to develop communities and citizens that are able to recognize the importance of understanding self, other, and context, the stories in this book are a powerful way to awaken our collective consciousness. As a leadership studies educator, this book is a humbling reminder that where we are situated in the world matters, and it influences how we navigate the world, and how the world responds to us. This is a great resource for leadership studies as it prompts our emerging and future leaders to think deeply about the lived experiences others bring. Exposing leaders to these narratives is a necessary component of creating a responsive leadership practice that recognizes the importance of narratives and intercultural competence."
— **Dr. Nyasha M. GuramatunhuCooper, Assistant Professor of Leadership Studies, Kennesaw State University**

"*Green Card Youth Voices* records, preserves, and adds important context regarding the struggles and travels of families currently coming to our country. Though their origins may be different, their aspirations for a better life are the same as the millions who came before."
— **John R. Tibbetts, 2018 Georgia Teacher of the Year, Worth County High School**

"This book is essential reading for anyone who is seeking to learn and understand a snapshot of what immigrant families experience in their journey to their new home in America. I am so grateful these immigrant youth were willing to share their stories with us. Stories are important and can build bridges as we seek to understand the perspectives of others, and this is an amazing collection of reflections and experiences from some incredible young people in Atlanta. Our youth are the future of our society, and the stories, determination and goals reflected in this collection make me excited for the impact they will have in Atlanta and beyond."
— **Emily Laney, Chair, Coalition of Refugee Service Agencies and Metro Atlanta Regional Director, Lutheran Services of Georgia**

"We all have a story to tell, and all of those stories collectively make up the American story. This powerful book tells the very real stories of a brave group of immigrant students in Georgia— young people who came here afraid of a new world, but courageous enough to try to make the most of the opportunities they were given. Not only are their successes engaging and inspirational, but their honesty is also insightful and instructive. All who are interested in going beyond the headlines should read this book."
— **Richard Carvajal, President of Valdosta State University**

"At a time when the very survival of immigrants is being challenged and threatened every single day, this book *Green Card Youth Voices: Immigration Stories from an Atlanta High School* provides rays of hope and trust back into these vulnerable groups who came into this country to rebuild their lives and fulfill their American Dreams. The compilation of short interesting essays provides excellent examples of hopes and survival which also serve well toward community-based actions that are crucial at this moment in this country."

—**Madhuri Sharma, Associate Professor, Department of Geography, University of Tennessee, Knoxville**

"*Green Card Youth Voices: Immigration Stories from an Atlanta High School* is a thoughtful collection that will inspire and empower you to challenge your convictions and broaden your horizons. It helps us see the world as a much smaller place and our place in a much larger light."

—**Seneca Vaught, Editor, Afro-Americans in New York Life and History, Author of *Is College a Lousy Investment?: Negotiating the Hidden Costs of Higher Education***

"What an extraordinary collection of human stories! The dreams of these young people ought to be the dreams of every American. They represent the best of our country. *Green Card Youth Voices* is a must-read for the supporter and the skeptic alike."

—**Lawrence Schall, President of Oglethorpe University**

"*Green Card Youth Voices* is a must-read book for educators and those working with immigrant youth. These powerful stories remind us of the humanity of the immigration story told through the eyes of young immigrant youth. In a time when the immigrant narrative is portrayed in a negative light, these are the voices that we should be hearing!"

—**Dr. Sanjuana Rodriguez, Assistant Professor of Reading and Literacy Education, Kennesaw State University**

"*Green Card Youth Voices* places real names and real stories into what has become a nameless and faceless immigration debate. This is essential reading for anyone who wants to understand what is at stake with immigration especially students in the 21st Century."

—**Ernie Lee, 2016 Georgia Teacher of the Year, Savannah-Chatham County Public School**

"What an honor to have our students recognized in a book of this caliber. Clarkston High School, one of the most diverse schools in the country, is pleased to be in partnership with Green Card Voices as they capture some of the unique stories for our community. While there are so many untold stories from our diverse population, the highlighted students, Farhat and Marie, have shared their stories in their own voice. They make us proud! Their lived experiences and perseverance embody what we treasure most about our school, our staff, and our students. Diversity comes to life as you read the pages of this book and "see" who we are."

—**Dr. Michelle E. Jones, Principal of Clarkston High School**

"Corners Outreach has worked for almost a decade to empower our community through education and fair job opportunities. We share in Brene Brown's belief: "People are hard to hate close-up." *Green Card Youth Voices* does an excellent job of allowing the reader to walk with teens in our community through their incredible stories of hardship, struggle, victory, and love. This is a fantastic, straightforward, and honest book."

—**Larry Campbell, Executive Director, Corners Outreach**

"*Green Card Youth Voices* beautifully captures the poignancy and power of young immigrants telling their own stories. Their courage is inspiring and their enthusiasm for their new country is a timely reminder of how the United States is enriched by the immigrant experience."

—**Ali Noorani, Executive Director, National Immigration Forum**

"*Green Card Youth Voices: Immigration Stories from an Atlanta High School* is a more than welcome addition to scholarship exploring the reception, settlement, and integration of immigrant newcomers in America. Prioritizing the voice and personal narratives of youth who represent a broad spectrum of backgrounds and experiences, the project offers a rich and resounding perspective that significantly enriches our understanding of the complex dynamics of the 21st-Century immigrant experience in Atlanta and beyond. At once heartbreaking and inspirational, *Green Card Youth Voices* is an extraordinary initiative that should be required reading and watching for any educator, researcher, policy maker, or civic leader working to make our cities and communities more welcoming and inclusive."

—Heather A. Smith, Professor of Geography and Co-Director of the Receptivity, Integration and Settlement in New Gateways (RISING) Research Group, University of North Carolina at Charlotte

"I am Jason Heard, the proud principal of the most culturally diverse high school in the State of Georgia: Cross Keys High School. We are truly the mecca of cultures that run a span of over 65 countries and 75 languages. Wholeheartedly, we embrace the fact that our students come to Cross Keys High School each and every day with a unique set of experiences and languages. I am both humbled and proud to know that irrespective of their native country of origin, the instructional language of achievement, beating the odds and perseverance are universal. Consistently, I aim to provide our students at Cross Keys High School with a canvas upon which to write their own life story. The *Green Card Youth Voice*s book is truly an extension of my vision of building bridges and respecting the cultures that each student represents. Students, I applaud you for sharing your journey with us. My best to you, always."

—Jason C. Heard, Principal, Cross Keys High School

"A diverse workforce is crucial for our economy and the future of our state. *Green Card Youth Voices* highlights the contributions of exemplary young immigrants from the Atlanta area who will form a critical and inspirational part of the state's economic backbone and help build a Georgia that is strong and vibrant."

—Santiago Marquez, President and CEO, Georgia Hispanic Chamber

"Real, powerful, and a timely book. It should be included as a piece of contemporary literature at every high school language arts class. *Green Card Youth Voices* gives a voice to so many silent young immigrants who dream to become part of society and pursue their own American Dream."

—Maria Paula Prieto, Family and Community Engagement Manager, Cobb County School District

"Powerful, practical, and solid advice on immigration from each personal story shared with confidence from the students. The students' expertise will change the way you think about immigration and will empower you to want to make a change in our country on how others view immigration. These stories gave me chills as I read them trying to imagine what they have gone through. This book is a game changer!"

—James B. Stinchcomb, CEO of Baux Blue Consulting

"*Green Card Youth Voices* puts a timely and necessary human face on a debate that all too often forgets that we are talking about real human beings and individual stories. What is remarkable about the young men and women profiled in this book is not only their struggles but also their resiliency and unshakeable faith in this country. These are young people we should be embracing, rather than demonizing, because what they hope to do and want to contribute will help all Americans in the future."

—Janet Murguía, President and CEO of UnidosUS, formerly the National Council of La Raza

"Sublime and riveting, *Green Card Youth Voices: Immigration Stories from an Atlanta High School* gives a valuable insight into the youth immigrant experience in the city with the nation's second highest growing immigrant population. Stories of 15 different origins take the reader on journey to discover the unrelenting power of hope and courage and connect us all to the universal human struggle to realize our dreams. It is a much-needed spotlight on the power, talent, and grit of our immigrant neighbors and a powerful reminder of the value they add to our communities. It is a must-read for anyone who craves to gain a holistic understanding of our City that like our nation was in part built, maintained, and made great by immigrants."

—Luisa F. Cardona, Atlanta Resident and Community Activist

"*Green Card Youth Voices* is a compelling compilation of personal stories of young people with aspirations of a brighter future. It captures the resilience, courage, and determination of the immigrant story—the American story of opportunities and possibilities. Green Card Voices gives credence to the lived experience of immigrants in a relevant and pivotal moment in our nation's history. These are the stories of courage and hope of those who dare to defy the odds and pursue their dreams—the American Dream . . . that anyone is welcome and anyone can make it in America."

—Karen C. Goff, Vice President for Student Affairs, Agnes Scott College

"There is nothing more important to society than ensuring that our children have both the ability to Hope and Dream. This book is really about the ability of the children of immigrants to both Hope and Dream. All of us must ensure a future that is available to each immigrant child that will allow them to take the sacrifice of their parents, who like all parents simply want a better life and opportunity for their children, and shape it into a grander, more expansive vision of their own futures. These are indeed the stories of the future of America, and we have never been in better hands."

—Charles H. Kuck, Managing Partner for Kuck | Baxter Immigration

"I applaud these immigrant high school students for telling their stories of innocence, struggle, and triumph. The details from these students' stories put flesh on the bones of diversity and what it means to be multicultural and multilingual today. No matter the pain they felt or pressure they endured, their lives birthed a purposeful piece of work! After reading the personal essays, I thought of all English Learner educators who speak the language of equity and seek to unify their English Learners, their organizations, and their community members with the threads of diversity. Those educators' persistent and consistent efforts have improved the lives of their immigrant and refugee students, have contributed to global workforce development, and have equipped immigrants to contribute to their societies. As an English for Speakers of Other Languages teacher, I am proud and humbled to raise my voice in unity with immigrants and refugees in Georgia, our Nation, and our world! All key stakeholders should read this book, share copies with their clientele, customers, and constituents, and use the insight gained from the personal essays to be an advocates and agents of change in their community!"

—Kendra M. Castelow, President,
Georgia Affiliate of Teachers of English to Speakers of Other Languages (Georgia TESOL)

"Powerful, compelling, and creatively assembled personal stories of perseverance, endurance, and courage that expand our knowledge, awareness, and understanding of immigration and the life journeys of thirty high school students in Atlanta, Georgia. *Green Card Youth Voices: Immigration Stories from an Atlanta High School* is itself the result of an amazing community engagement partnership involving university faculty and community organizations. The stories and interviews will serve as powerful teaching and learning tools for use inside and outside classrooms here in the US and abroad."

—Dr. Robert H. "Robin" Dorff, Dean of the College of Humanities and Social Sciences,
Kennesaw State University

Green Card Youth Voices

Immigration Stories from an Atlanta High School

Marie Nikuze, Hau Phuong Vo, Kumba Njie, Mario, Nu
Nu, Abdoulaye Diallo, HM Sakib, Dim Cing, Daniel, Sean
Cordovez, Dania Karim, Luis, Farhat Sadat, Edanur Isik,
Sanjith Yadav, America, May Da, Eliyas Sala, Karelin,
Faysal Ando, Yehimi Cambrón

Authors

Tea Rozman Clark, Darlene Xiomara Rodriguez, Lara Smith-Sitton
Editors

ISBN 13: 978-0-9974960-6-2
LCCN: 2018932723

Printed in the United States of America
First Printing: 2018
20 19 18 17 16   5 4 3 2 1

Edited by Tea Rozman Clark, Darlene Xiomara Rodriguez, Lara Smith-Sitton

Cover design by Elena Dodevska
Interior design by José Guzmán

Photography, videography by Media Active: Youth Produced Media
Illustrations by Yehimi Cambrón

Wise Ink Creative Publishing
837 Glenwood Ave.
Minneapolis, MN 55405
www.wiseinkpub.com

We dedicate this book to all people whose voices have been silenced, and we hope the time will come when all human beings will be able to share their stories without fear.

Table of Contents

Foreword — i
Acknowledgments — iii
Introduction — ix
Georgia Maps — xiv
How to Use this Book — xvii
World Map — xviii
Personal Essays — xxi

    Marie Nikuze—Rwanda — 1
    Hau Phuong Vo—Vietnam — 5
    Kumba Njie—The Gambia — 9
    Mario—Mexico — 15
    Nu Nu—Myanmar — 19
    Abdoulaye Diallo—Guinea — 23
    HM Sakib—Bangladesh — 31
    Dim Cing—Myanmar — 39
    Daniel—Mexico — 43
    Sean Cordovez—Philippines — 47
    Dania Karim—Bangladesh — 53
    Luis—Mexico — 57
    Farhat Sadat—Afghanistan — 65
    Edanur Isik—Turkey — 69
    Sanjith Yadav—Nepal — 75
    America—Mexico — 79
    Eliyas Sala—Ethiopia — 83
    May Da—Myanmar — 89
    Karelin—Guatemala — 93
    Faysal Ando—Ethiopia — 99
    Yehimi Cambrón—Mexico — 105

Afterword — 113
Study Guide — 115
Glossary — 119
About the Advisory Team — 126
About Green Card Voices — 127

Foreword

One day last year, I had a senior come into my room asking for a book. All students are required to read books outside their regular classroom assignments and then present to the whole school. He was overwhelmed with college applications, attending dual enrollment college classes, and the pressures of being the first in his family to graduate from high school. I handed him one of the *Green Card Youth Voices* books and said, "I think you'll like this. It's pretty easy, plus my friend compiled it." He is a reluctant reader at best, but he came into my office a week later saying he completed it and couldn't wait to present to the rest of his schoolmates. At the end of the presentation he said, "I would recommend this book to all the students here and everywhere because it made me feel normal. I didn't feel alone. I laughed, and I cried, and I think all of you here should read it."

My connection to Green Card Voices first happened when I met Tea Rozman Clark in 2016 at the Executive Program in Social Entrepreneurship at Stanford University. In a group of fifty-six young ambitious CEOs and executives spanning non-profits, b-corps, and social ventures, we were the only two directly working with refugees and immigrants. I was running the first accredited school dedicated to refugee education in the country and was looking for ways to grow. She was the executive director of a nonprofit dedicated to sharing stories of first-generation immigrants and refugees. We bonded over our passion and determination to humanize the refugee experience. Our organizations shared similar obstacles, but we both also held the belief in the power of youth—their resilience and determination. Our kids had something unique to offer America, a perspective and deeper appreciation for everything that we take for granted in this country.

In 2012, I was a new American citizen voting in my first election ever. Growing up in the Middle East, I didn't have the right to vote. I gained my American citizenship in the fall of 2011. When *CBS News Sunday Morning* approached me to do a story on my work, I agreed knowing that it was important to share our stories; I was also very lucky that their filming coincided with my citizenship test and swearing-in ceremony. The response we received was overwhelming, solidifying my belief in the power of storytelling the ability of a story to touch hearts and change minds.

Our stories need to be told. Our voices need to be heard. Our experiences should not be used as political tools but should serve as ways that we can humanize each other.

When I decided to share my story on the TED Talks stage in April 2017, I knew that my toughest audience would be those who knew me best. I shared publicly for the first time that I am a child of refugees, that I am gay, and that I have received political asylum. When I showed the talk to the students, I was nervous about their response. I had to leave the room as they watched. Later, they told me they loved it. But what stays with me is the shy kid who came up to me at the end of the day and said, "You made me feel proud to be a refugee, Coach. Thank you."

Our school has a deep commitment to empowering students through stories and their own refugee identities. We do so by embedding their experiences throughout the curriculum. In high school, students are reading stories about the refugee experience like *What is the What* and *Zeitoun* by Dave Eggers. We include immigrant authors like Ishmael Beah, Jhumpa Lahiri, and Viet Thanh Nguyen. And in my office, I keep the different Green Card Voices books. Students often come in asking for book recommendations, and I point them toward Green Card Voices' incredible collections of experiences, voices, and stories.

Now, in the classroom, we use stories from the *Green Card Youth Voices* collections alongside with other books, such as *A Long Way Gone* and *The Great Gatsby*. These powerful student stories show resilience and, most importantly, each story is told by a unique and original voice. At a time in our country when we do not listen enough, these books are an opportunity for us to listen to the kids—their voices, their experiences—and to understand how uniquely American their stories are.

Luma Mufleh
Founder and CEO of Fugees Family, Inc.; Head Coach of the Fugees Soccer Teams

Acknowledgments

To make this book possible, we have many people, organizations, and entities to thank.

The most important people in this project are the twenty-one authors who so courageously shared their worlds. From hours of preparation in the classroom to bravely telling their stories on camera, from posing for portraits to working with Kennesaw State University (KSU) faculty and students to polish their essays, these young people have put forth tremendous effort in order to bring you these essays and video narratives. They are the heart and soul of this work, and they represent the very heart and soul of America. We thank you and are incredibly proud of you!

DeKalb County Public Schools joins us in our collective pride, from the superintendent's office, to the English Language facilitators and educators, and to the principals who lead each of the schools these young authors attend. We would like to thank Superintendent R. Stephen Green, Principal Yul Royce Toombs (DeKalb International Student Center, DISC), Principal Jason Heard (Cross Keys High School, CKHS), and Principal Michelle Jones (Clarkston High School, CHS).

Our gratitude is multiplied to our school-site partners who helped us identify, recruit, orient, and prepare students for this work. Without your commitment to these authors and to this project, this book would not have been possible. Our honor roll of educators has you at the top of the list: Jan Anglade (DISC), Jacob Eismeier (CKHS), and Julie Goldberg (CHS). Your enthusiasm for this project has not waivered—if anything, it has only strengthened throughout this experience. We are fortunate to have you guiding young people from all walks of life through public education.

To enter into a community, especially a school-based setting with vulnerable immigrant youth, one needs to have the support of key partners. We were fortunate to find this in the Latin American Association (LAA). Their endorsement for this project, including serving as a co-investigator on a grant that provided the initial funding, was invaluable. Similarly, they aided us at critical points throughout the project by working with the DACA (Deferred Action for Childhood Arrivals) recipients so that they would be supported during a time of great uncertainty. The strong reputation of the

LAA in Atlanta and throughout the southeastern US has been a great asset to the project. We would like to thank Eliezer Vélez, Managing Director of Education; David Schaefer, Managing Director of Advocacy; Aníbal Torres, Executive Director; and the entire LAA Staff for the privilege of working with and alongside of them.

To capture the authors' stories in their own words, the stories were first recorded on film. While Green Card Voices' (GCV) Executive Director, Tea Rozman Clark interviewed the immigrant students, GCV also contracted with Media Active to film the interviews and take the portraits. Media Active is a youth-produced media production studio based in Minneapolis/St. Paul that provides teens and young adults with opportunities to gain valuable re-al-world job training and experience by creating professional-quality media products. The beautiful photographs and raw video footage are credited to David Buchanan, DeAundre Dent, and Michael Hay.

We would like to thank the Green Card Voices team. In specific, José Guzmán, Graphic Designer and Video Editor, transformed raw video footage into compelling digital narratives and designed the interior of the book. Rachel Mueller, Program Manager, did an extraordinary job of keeping the team on track, on task, and on time to ensure the project's success. The "can-do attitude" both have had throughout this journey has been absolutely amazing. We are thankful that Zamzam Ahmed joined the team as Program Associate and are excited to have her support for future programming. Additionally, we thank Zaynab Abdi, Immigrant and Refugee Youth Ambassador, who came to Atlanta to meet with each author in this volume to speak about a range of topics, including her immigrant experience, her role as an author in the first GCV book and experience as a Malala Fund Delegate. We extend deep gratitude to Dr. Tea Rozman Clark, GCV Co-Founder and Executive Director, whose vision and leadership allowed for transformational educational experiences for all involved. Her grace and commitment is inspiring. And finally, to the Board of Directors for supporting us in bringing Green Card Voices to Georgia to make Atlanta the launch pad for the organization, increasing its national reach and presence.

In equal measure we must show appreciation to and for the KSU partners in this ensemble. Our deep gratitude goes to Dr. Darlene Xiomara Rodriguez, Assistant Professor of Social Work and Human Services, for her enthusiasm, energy, commitment, and advocacy that has given this book the necessary context and partnerships in Atlanta to make it a success. We also cannot thank enough Dr. Lara Smith-Sitton, Director of Community Engagement and Assistant Professor of English, who shepherded an amazing team of KSU students doing critical editing work, in addition to providing extensive expertise of her own. We are infinitely grateful to them both! The Office of Diversity and Inclusion and the Division of Global Affairs provided us with the initial financial provisions needed to realize our vision. This allowed the the Office of Community Engagement, (under Brian Wooten and Kimberly Henghold's leadership), the LAA, and us to have the financial footing and university resources to confidently move forward in our community-university partnership to work on this project.

To accomplish this, an interdisciplinary team of faculty were brought together from three different colleges—WellStar College of Health and Human Services, College of Humanities and Social Sciences, and Bagwell College of Education—to provide subject-matter expertise and oversight. Additionally, they were instrumental in brokering connections among various community organizations, facilitating local project logistics in the Atlanta area, and being present at each of the schools when we were on site. We especially want to thank two exceptional collaborators: Dr. Paul N. McDaniel, Assistant Professor of Geography, for his dedication to this project as well as for creating the maps that depict where the foreign-born population resides in Atlanta and Georgia and Dr. Sanjuana Rodriguez, Assistant Professor of Education, for serving as a sounding board regarding DACA's liminal state and how best to move forward with the aim of doing no harm but doing great good in telling these young people's stories.

But much like the authors in this book whose stories are told, we need to congratulate and recognize the contributions made by the KSU undergraduate and graduate students who helped bring these stories to life. We would like to thank Jennifer Bledsoe, from the Social Work and Human Services Department, who worked with us during the first phase of the project, which included identifying, orienting, and preparing the authors for their interviews. During phase two, twenty-five students in English and the professional writing program transcribed the narratives and later worked as developmental editors one-on-one with the authors to help them compose their personal essays. They served as copy editors, researchers, and proofreaders to support the additional needs of the collection. The student editors include Katherine Adamson, Katie Andrews, Mazie Beavers, Ariel Beedles, Courtney Bradford, Allyson Brooks, Cydni Cope, Kimberlyn Donnelly, Destinee

Easton, Tessa Hilton, Emily Jobe, Caysea Ledford, Abi Marmurowicz, Jennifer McNaughton, Kyle Proshek, Emma Rice, Alem Sahic, Lacy Smith, Conner Sutton, Jordan Swanson, and McKenna Wood. Special acknowledgement also to Allison Dobo, Kelsey Medlin, Stephen Oweida, and Estefany Palacio, who worked with the student authors and continued to provide further support as editorial team leaders through internships with the English Department. We hope this experience carries you forward in your personal and professional lives as you model how to treat, speak, and write about people with dignity and respect.

The KSU community-university partnership strengthened community relationships, applied research, and teaching, which embodies why KSU received the Carnegie Foundation's Community Engagement Classification. It also raised the university's profile as a campus that seeks to increase international education, global community engagement, and intercultural scholarship between the KSU community and the community-at-large. Therefore, we thank the KSU departmental colleagues, chairpersons, and deans for being amazingly supportive of Rodriguez and Smith-Sitton as individuals and as a collective to bring this volume together.

Beyond KSU, we would like to thank the members of the Georgia Immigration Research Network who wrote or helped us obtain numerous endorsements for this edited volume. Thank you for the work that you do in the public, private, and nonprofit sectors to inform and improve immigrant integration throughout Georgia—may this book be a tool that will bolster our collective goal!

Special thanks to our foreword author, Luma Mufleh, who prefaced these young people's stories with reflections of her own immigrant experience. As founder of the nonprofit organization "The Fugees" (Fugee Family, Inc.) which is devoted to working with child survivors of war, Mufleh has been a trailblazer in the refugee resettlement movement throughout the US, and especially in Clarkston, Georgia. Thus, it is especially fitting to have her write this forward on the heels of her own book being released and a motion picture in the works that chronicles the Clarkston community and the lives of this small town with a big heart.

It is our honor to have commissioned artist Yehimi Cambrón to illustrate the portraits of the authors who are DACA recipients. She developed a process through which these authors were involved in ways that valued them as individuals and strived to be collaborative, ensuring that the six authors are satisfied with the way they are represented. With her artistic skills and undeniable commitment to the authors' voices, we were able to move mountains to make this storytelling project come to life!

A tremendous thank you goes to Dara Beevas and Patrick Maloney at Wise Ink Creative Publishing for their advice, support, and encouragement. Our collaboration as well as their donations of time and consultation through the InkPossible program greatly enhanced the final product.

Thank you to Veronica Quillien who designed the study guide and who is also the lead author of *Voices of Immigrant Storytelling: Teaching Guide for Middle and High Schools*. She is a first-generation immigrant herself and is a PhD student in the Curriculum and Instruction Department at the University of Minnesota. We thank her for her expertise.

To Marlon A. Walker of the *Atlanta Journal-Constitution*, Evelyn Andrews of Reporter Newspapers, and R. Scott Belzer of *The DeKalb Free Press* for seeing the value in these students' words and creating media—thank you for helping us spread the word.

A huge thank you to Christopher Moses, the Dan Reardon Director of Education and Associate Artistic Director, for partnering with us on the the venue for our book launch celebration at the Alliance Theater. Upon publication of the book, the students will be able to celebrate their publishing achievements and be publicly recognized because of this partnership.

Thank you to all of the present Green Card Voices board members— Jessica Cordova Kramer, Johan Eriksson, Masami Suga, George C. Maxwell, Hibo Abdi, Tara Kennedy, Ruben Hidalgo, Dana Boyle, Gregory Eagan IV, Debjyoti Dwivedy, and Mahlet Aschenaki—and past board members—Miguel Ramos, Veronica Quillien, Katie Murphy-Olsen, Jane Graupman, Ali Alizadeh, Laura Danielson, Jeff Corn, Ruhel Islam, Angela Eifert, Matt Kim, and Kathy Seipp—and all others who have helped our mission along the way.

Finally, and most personally, we would like to thank our spouses, children, families, and friends for helping each of us put our passion to use for the betterment of society.

With the above support Green Card Voices is truly able to realize its mission to use the art of storytelling to build bridges between immigrant and non-immigrants communities by sharing first-hand immigration stories of foreign-born Americans. Our aim is to help the collective us in the US see each "wave of immigrants" as individuals with assets and strengths that make America remarkable.

Introduction

The American landscape and culture since its founding has always been a mixture of races, ethnicities, and cultures that together create a stronger and more vibrant country. This narrative must also include the Native Americans whose land we now inhabit, and the descendants of the Africans who were forcibly brought here. According to the US Census Bureau, an estimated 13.4% of our population in 2015, or 43.2 million people, were not born in the United States, and immigration to the United States is increasing—by 2050, one in five Americans will be an immigrant.[1] This is not unusual, as the United States has enjoyed similar periods of immigration, which strengthened our country through growth and development.

This book will introduce you to young people who live in the crosshairs of the immigration debate, who live and grow and plan for their futures even as an uncertain political climate and negative immigration rhetoric dominates our media, our politics, and, sometimes, our dinner table conversations. The local stories we gather here are unique and specific yet are illustrative of the breadth of the immigrant experience. In this book, immigrant youth share their hopes and dreams, which often includes desires to make the United States a better place for all. Their aspirations should remind us of the achievements of earlier immigrants whose significant contributions shaped these United States.

Green Card Youth Voices: Immigration Stories from an Atlanta High School is Green Card Voices' fourth youth anthology. The first book, based in Minneapolis, Minnesota, was published in May 2016 and featured thirty personal essays written by immigrant high school students from thirteen different countries. Receiving the Gold Medal Award for Best Multicultural Non-Fiction Chapter Book from the Moonbeam Children's Book Awards, it is assigned reading at more than 150 schools. This collection serves as the template for our success. We collected an additional sixty stories from young people in Fargo, North Dakota and St. Paul, Minnesota, which became two additional youth anthologies based in each of these cities.

With *Green Card Youth Voices: Immigration Stories from an Atlanta High School*, we've traveled outside the Midwest for the first time, expanding our programming nationally to an area that could greatly benefit from this type of resource. Green Card Voices and our collaborators work every day to uplift stories of immigrants, refugees, and their families in order for all to be welcomed here.

1. López, G. and Radford, J. (2017, May). Facts on US Immigrants, 2015: Statistical Portrait of the Foreign Born Population in the United States. Pew Research Center: Hispanic Trends. Retrieved from www.pewhispanic.org/2017/05/03/facts-on-u-s-immigrants-current-data/

Our mission is to use the art of storytelling to combat stereotypes and create empathy. We do this through our online video platform, our book collections, and teaching guides that help teachers instruct students by using real-life immigrant stories as well as traveling exhibits that create physical spaces where the immigrant journeys have a powerful visual impact.

Often referred to as the "Capital of the South," Atlanta is city with a deep history of both racial segregation and civil rights reform. For many decades, Georgia lived within a black/white "bi-chromatic" paradigm, yet in recent years it has undergone a seismic demographic shift. In fact, the Atlanta metropolitan area is one of six "major emerging" new immigrant gateways in the United States[2]—areas that have not historically received many immigrants but where foreign-born populations are now growing extremely swiftly[3]. According to the Atlanta Regional Commission's State of the Region Report (2015), the region is now "home to the 10th largest regional economy in the United States."[4] The foreign-born individuals who call Georgia home are responsible for a significant amount of this economic growth. Nearly one-in-five self-employed business owners in Georgia and in the Atlanta metropolitan area is an immigrant. While only 10% of Georgia residents are immigrants, almost 14% of Georgia's workforce are immigrants.[5]

The high schools we chose for this book shared similar characteristics: all have a high percentage of immigrant students, and as a group, they reflect broader immigration trends in Georgia. While the students featured in each of the Green Card Voices' earlier books all attended the same high school in the specified city, this volume includes students and one teacher who attend or teach at three separate schools in the Atlanta area, specifically in DeKalb County. DeKalb County is the fourth most-populous county in Georgia with nearly 750,000 residents, of which 16% are foreign-born.[6] Consequently, the first place an immigrant newcomer would likely matriculate for school is the DeKalb International Student Center (DeKalb International).

DeKalb International is a newcomer school, a common institution in large school districts throughout the state. Geared toward preparing immigrants

2. Other major-emerging gateways that have only recently become major destinations for immigrants include Austin, TX; Charlotte, NC; Las Vegas, NV; Orlando, FL; and Phoenix, AZ.

3. Singer, A. (2015, December). A Typology of Immigrant Gateways, 2014. Metropolitan Policy Program. Brookings Institute. Retrieved from www.brookings.edu/wp-content/uploads/2016/07/Gateways-2014-update-1.pdf

4. Atlanta Regional Commission. (2015, May). The Introduction to the Region's Plan: An Assessment of the Atlanta Region. Retrieved from documents.atlantaregional.com/The-Atlanta-Region-s-Plan/RegionalAssessmentRevised_2015_05_07.pdf

5. New American Economy (2016, August). The Contributions of New Americans in Georgia. Retrieved from www.newamericaneconomy.org/wp-content/uploads/2017/02/nae-ga-report.pdf

6. TownCharts. (2017, December). DeKalb County Population Charts. DeKalb County, Georgia Demographics Data. Retrieved from www.towncharts.com/Georgia/Demographics/DeKalb-County-GA-Demographics-data.html

for integration into schools in their home districts, the school provides outreach and engagement to parents who may not speak English as well as intensive English training for students and substantive academic assessment. DeKalb International also serves Students with Limited and Interrupted Formal Education (SLIFE). SLIFE students may not have been able to attend school in their home countries or have had their formal schooling interrupted for a variety of reasons; thus, they often require additional assistance to achieve the learning fundamentals needed for successful matriculation to mainstream, neighborhood schools. Because of the diverse backgrounds of those enrolled, students can stay at DeKalb International for as short as one semester and as long as two years before transferring to local schools in their district.

Clarkston High School is one of the neighborhood schools immigrants often move to after DeKalb International. Located in the City of Clarkston—a city recognized as the "Ellis Island of the South" and described by *Atlanta* magazine as the "most diverse square mile in America."[7] Clarkston students come from more than fifty-four countries and bringing at least forty-eight different languages. It is considered the most culturally and ethnically diverse school in the DeKalb County School System. Cross Keys High School is the other feeder school for many DeKalb International students. Cross Keys is located in the City of Brookhaven, a suburb that is located northeast of Atlanta. Cross Keys' student composition is 80% Hispanic, 11% Black, 6% Asian, 1% White, and less than 1% other racial groups, including those identifying with two or more races.

The authors in the Atlanta book, from these three schools, represent a range of experiences and backgrounds—from new-arrivals to graduating seniors, from refugees to Green Card holders and even US citizens. They are the emerging educators, business owners, elected officials, and community leaders that will shape the Atlanta region and the southeastern United States in the foreseeable future. These young people are wise beyond their years, and our communities will greatly benefit from their shared experiences.

The process of creating this book was specifically designed to meet the needs of the young immigrant authors. Many have had limited or interrupted education. For these reasons, we recorded the authors speaking their stories before we ever approached the page. Then, in the spirit of the educational and civic engagement opportunities created by our work, we continued the tradition of community engagement by partnering with area universities, professors, and students to create community-writing and service learning experiences that expand the reach of these stories. In line with this, the narratives were transcribed by a

7. Shaer, M. (2017, January). Ellis Island South: Welcome to the Most Diverse Square Mile in America. Atlanta Magazine. Retrieved from www.atlantamagazine.com/great-reads/ellis-island-south-welcome-diverse-square-mile-america/

group of undergraduate and graduate student editors from Kennesaw State University, who then worked with the immigrant authors to develop and polish their essays while retaining each student's unique voice. At every step of the way, the immigrant authors were in control of their narratives, and what you read within these pages and watch in the videos reflect immense bravery.

Bravery is what is required to share these stories, as book comes forward in challenging times for immigrants in the US. In 2017 and today, different segments from the immigrant community face unique challenges: the banning citizens of eight countries, most majority-Muslim, from entering the United States; reducing refugee admissions to the lowest levels since the creation of the resettlement program in 1980; and canceling the Deferred Action for Childhood Arrivals (DACA) program, affecting 800,000 immigrants brought to the United States as minor children.[8]

In April 2017, when we first started discussing doing a book in Atlanta, we were committed to including the stories of DACA recipients, also known as "Dreamers," in order to show the full breadth of immigrant experiences present in Atlanta. Currently there are over 21,000 young people with DACA status in Georgia, which provides legal authorization to work and stay in the United States.[9] In September 2017, six months into the presidency of the new administration, we began identifying and working with twenty-seven young immigrants, including six DACA recipients (five students and one former student who is now a teacher at Cross Keys High School). This was the first time we interviewed "Dreamers" for one of the book projects. As of the writing and the publication of this book, however, the administration and the US Congress have not found a permanent solution for DACA holders; therefore, the future status of all DACA recipients is uncertain. In order to protect the six DACA recipients in this book, for this book's first edition, the Green Card Voices team elected to include drawn portraits of each of these individuals, instead of photo portraits, and we use only their first names. We believe this is a thoughtful and novel approach. Notably, the drawn portraits are the work of artist Yehimi Cambrón, an author in this book and a "Dreamer" herself. The drawn portraits include monarch butterflies, a widely used symbol for immigration.[10] We believe this approach honors our values to share these important narratives, while responsibly and mindfully considering the individual situations of the authors.

Now more than ever, Green Card Voices and other organizations that

8. US Citizenship and Immigration Services. (n.d.) Consideration of Deferred Action for Childhood Arrivals (DACA). Retrieved from www.uscis.gov/archive/consideration-deferred-action-childhood-arrivals-daca

9. Migration Policy Institute. (n.d.) Deferred Action for Childhood Arrivals (DACA) Data Tools. Retrieved from www.migrationpolicy.org/programs/data-hub/deferred-action-childhood-arrivals-daca-profiles

10. In North America, monarch butterflies migrate north and south on an annual basis

help share the stories of immigrants have a role to play to expand our understanding of the immigrant experience and to highlight the contributions made by this powerful community. To uphold our country's founding principles of liberty, justice, equality, and dignity for all, we must remember that with diverse newcomers comes growth and opportunity.

Within Georgia, there are seven municipalities that have identified themselves as "welcoming cities"—Atlanta, Brookhaven, Clarkston, Decatur, East Point, Norcross, and Stockbridge.[11] Each of these cities, by virtue of their elected, business, nonprofit, and community leaders, have made a commitment to work together to create a welcoming community climate that supports long-term integration. They are equally committed to helping newcomers and long-time residents find common ground and shared leadership opportunities that will help communicate and sustain long-term economic and social integration of newcomers. These cities, along with several nonprofit partners, have embarked on creating a "One Region Initiative" with the non-profit organization Welcoming America in order to grow this effort throughout the Atlanta Metropolitan Statistical Area and become a model for other regions throughout the country. We hope that this book is one more way of inspiring the same spirit of openness and inclusion.

We believe sharing stories is a powerful tool that can help us reach the goal of a fully integrated and compassionate society. Stories not only empower the teller, whose life experiences and unique contributions become valuable and validated through sharing, but they also educate the broader public and help us see how we all share the experience of being human. We hope you will be as moved as we are by the stories in this book. These writers came to America, as generations have, seeking a place where they could breathe the free air, live life with dignity, and enjoy equal justice under the law. It is our job to build a society of compassion and hope, worthy to be the garden in which their treasured dreams can grow. We hope that reading about the memories, realities, and hopes of these twenty-one young people will inspire you. Their courage shows that the future of Atlanta—and indeed America itself—is in good hands.

Tea Rozman Clark, PhD
Rachel Mueller
Green Card Voices

Darlene Xiomara Rodriguez, PhD
Lara Smith-Sitton, PhD
Kennesaw State University

---

11. Welcoming America (n.d.). Our Network. Retrieved from www.welcomingamerica.org/programs/our-network

Georgia Maps

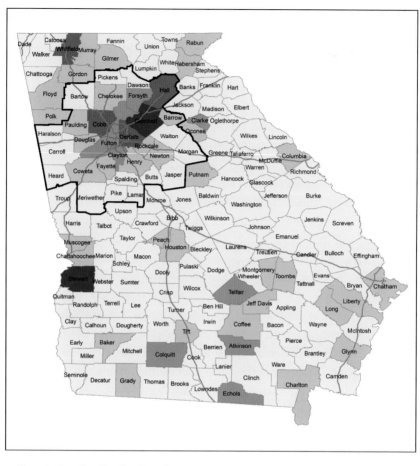

Georgia Counties, Foreign-Born Percent, 2016

- 5 percent or under
- 5.1 to 10 percent
- 10.1 to 15 percent
- 15.1 to 20 percent
- Over 20 percent

0   25   50   75   100
Miles
— Interstate Highways
County Boundary
Atlanta MSA Boundary

This map illustrates the percent of each Georgia county's total population that is foreign-born in 2016. Data are from the *2016 American Community Survey* five-year estimates from the US Census Bureau. Cartography by Dr. Paul McDaniel in the Department of Geography and Anthropology at Kennesaw State University.

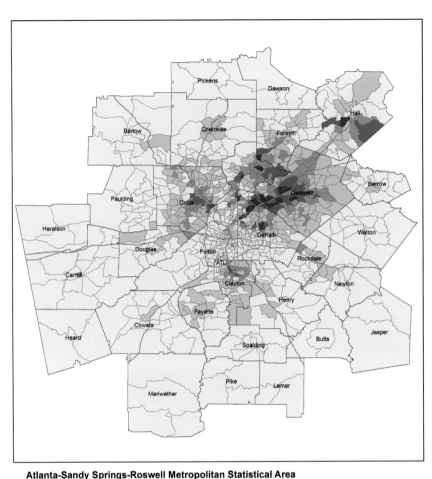

**Atlanta-Sandy Springs-Roswell Metropolitan Statistical Area
Census Tracts, Foreign-Born Percent, 2016**

10 percent or under

10.1 to 20 percent

20.1 to 30 percent

30.1 to 40 percent

Over 40 percent

0   9   18   27   36

Miles

—— Interstate Highways

County Boundary

ATL Atlanta Airport

This map illustrates the geography of foreign-born settlement in the Atlanta metro area. Specifically, the map shows the percent of each census tract's total population that is foreign-born in the Atlanta-Sandy Springs-Roswell Metropolitan Statistical Area (MSA) in 2016. Data are from the *2016 American Community Survey* five-year estimates from the US Census Bureau. Cartography by Dr. Paul McDaniel in the Department of Geography and Anthropology at Kennesaw State University.

How to Use this Book

At the end of each student's essay, you will find a URL link to that student's digital narrative on Green Card Voices' website. You will also see a QR code link to that story. Below are instructions for using your mobile device to scan a QR code.

1.Using your mobile device—such as a smartphone or tablet—visit the App Store for your network, such as the Apple Store or the Android Store. Search the App Store for a "QR reader." You will find multiple free apps for you to download, and any one of them will work with this book.

2.Open your new QR reader app. Once the app has opened, hover the camera on your mobile device a few inches away from the QR code you want to scan. The app will capture the image of the QR code and take you to that student's profile page on the Green Card Voices website.

3. Once your web browser opens, you'll see the digital story. Press play and watch one of our inspirational stories.

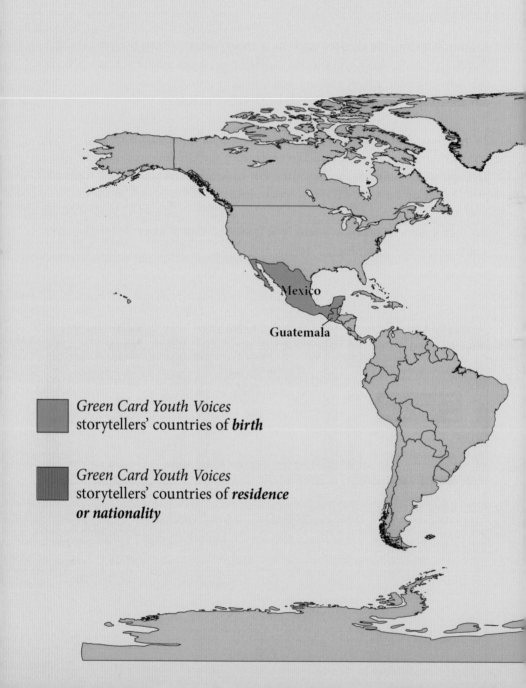

Mexico

Guatemala

Green Card Youth Voices
storytellers' countries of *birth*

Green Card Youth Voices
storytellers' countries of *residence
or nationality*

World Map

Turkey

Afghanistan
Nepal
Bhutan
Myanmar
(Burma)

Saudi
Arabia

India

Gambia

Senegal

Philippines

Bangladesh

Ethiopia

uinea

Rwanda

Malaysia

Democratic
Republic of the
Congo

Personal Essays

Kigali,
Rwanda

Marie Nikuze

From: Kigali, Rwanda
Current City: Atlanta, GA

"WE WENT IN THE FOREST SOMETIMES TO CUT FIREWOOD IN ORDER TO COOK FOOD. IF YOU DIDN'T HAVE MONEY YOU COULDN'T BUY CHARCOAL OR USE GAS FOR THE FIRE."

My name is Marie. I was born in Rwanda in 1999. My origin country is Democratic Republic of Congo. My parents moved to Rwanda, and I was born there. We lived in Rwanda twenty years ago. I lived with my parents and siblings in a camp. I have four sisters and three brothers. We all came to America. I don't know many things about my origin country, but my parents told me something about my country. There was more war; some people killed others. There was someone who tried to kill parents. They ran into the forest. Sometimes they slept in the forest, and in the morning they continued walking. My parents moved to Rwanda in 1996.

We lived there in the camp. We waited for food every month. That food was like maize and beans. Sometimes we got clothes to wear. We went in the forest sometimes to cut firewood in order to cook the food. If you didn't have money, you couldn't buy charcoal or use gas for the fire.

I had my friends there. I liked them. I lived with them all of my life. My school in Rwanda was very difficult. We studied and I stopped in grade nine. If your family didn't have money, you couldn't continue your school. If you got someone to help you continue and pay for your school, you could go to high school. Even if you finished school or someone helped you study for high school, you couldn't get a job because you were just a refugee, you were not a citizen. Also you couldn't study at university, as it's very expensive. That's why if you finished your school, you stayed at home, and you didn't have a job. That was very difficult. Also, if you finished university and didn't get a job, it was very difficult to live there. That is what I remember.

Someone came to choose a family from our camp. Sometimes they chose like ten families to interview. Some people from America came and over two years interviewed us many times. They were from American Refugee Committee. They asked us about our country. They asked us why we moved

1

to Rwanda; why we were not in our country; what life is like in camp. We told them about that. They chose America for us, and we left in 2015.

I was very happy because I thought I was going to change my life. I was going to continue my education. I was going to be great person. The other side was I was sad because I was going to leave my friend. My friend was sad because we were best friends.

When they told me to go to America, I packed everything I had, like clothes and shoes. They took us to Kigali. We stayed there one week. Then we took a plane and flew to Ethiopia. And then we took another plane to America. I don't know what countries we went over to get here. My parents were very nervous because it's their first time getting on an airplane. I was also very nervous. I was very scared because I thought we were going to get in an accident. My parents told me I don't have to be scared because there was a pilot. The pilot knew how to drive the plane. In the airplane, it was good because you got a restroom. We got food, drinks, whatever I needed. We were in the sky for like two days.

First when we got to America, we went to New Jersey. We stopped there but got on another plane. We took the other plane to Atlanta. I don't remember the places we went over to get to Atlanta, but it was the last flight I took to get here.

First time I got here, I saw everything was new, new for me. I was very scared. I saw many things I didn't see in camp. I saw many buildings. We didn't have buildings like them in Africa. I met with White people—first time in my life. Then I saw my people in America, and they smiled. They said we were funny, and I think they laughed at me because we were funny.

We got a case manager when we came to Atlanta. She was a Rwandan case manager. I like that because she spoke the same language as me. She helped us with everything we needed, and we were happy because we were scared. She gave us money. That money helped us buy food to eat. Everything we wanted, we told her, and she helped us. I didn't like American food because it was my first time eating that food, but we just ate it because we didn't know where the market was. We didn't know how to drive to get to the market.

My life in Africa and here are very different. In Africa, we had to find firewood to cook, but here we cook with the stove. Here, we have water in our home. We have a toilet inside our home. We use a car for everything, like for shopping, but in Africa, we walked.

I first went to DeKalb International School, and then I moved to this school. So, at DeKalb International School, I was very scared because I didn't know anyone there that was from my country that could speak my language. That made me sad because I couldn't speak with everyone because I didn't know enough English. But the next week, I got a friend who spoke my language. I kept my friend from another country, and I tried to use English with that friend. I am now at Clarkston High School. I am trying to learn English, so I can talk to everyone.

I've been in America eight months now. My life is very good because it's different from life in the camp. Now I eat whatever I want. I drink whatever I want. I make friends from my country and from other countries. I like to watch movies and to listen to music. I go to visit my friend sometimes. I have more friends now. I do sports like track. I go shopping, and on Sunday, I go to pray. It is very fun.

In the future, I want to be doctor, a child doctor. I want to help people in my country. I want to go to visit them. I need to know what happened with my friend after I separated. I want to help poor people there.

If I had stayed in Rwanda, I would finish my school, and then I would have stayed at home. I wouldn't a get job. Even if I got the opportunity, I wouldn't get a job because there are no jobs in camp. Some people stayed home after university because they were refugees and they couldn't get a job. We couldn't get a job because we are refugees, not citizens.

As my conclusion, I would like to tell American people there are refugees in different countries. Don't ignore that, because everything that happens in their countries, they didn't plan that. I would like to ask them to try to help poor people. Keep helping other people. I also need to thank the American government. Thank you for taking me out of the camp. Thank you for your help. Thank you so much. God bless you.

VIDEO LINKS

greencardvoices.org/speakers/marie-nikuze

Binh Duong,
Vietnam

Hau Phuong Vo

From: Binh Duong, Vietnam
Current City: Atlanta, GA

"THEY LAUGHED AT MY ACCENT. I WAS CONFUSED AND THOUGHT, "WHY DO THEY HAVE TO LAUGH AT ME?" JUST BECAUSE WE CAME FROM ANOTHER COUNTRY DIDN'T MEAN THEY HAD TO LAUGH AT ME."

I was born in Binh Duong, Vietnam, and it was a big city for me, even though Atlanta is bigger.

I had seven days of school from 7:00 am to 11:30 am, and then I got home and had tutorial from 2:00 pm to 3:00 pm. I had more tutorials at the teacher's house from 4:00 pm to 5:30 pm, and then I had judo practice from 6:00 pm to 8:00 pm. Then, I finally got home and had to prepare for the next day to do it all over again. I had to study for the next day of school because there's a lot of homework over there. More than over here. It usually took two hours to do the work, and some days, I had to wake up at 4:00 in the morning to do all of it. I only had free time on Sunday to go out to eat and drink with my friends. Even school was hard, but I love to be around my friends. They are friendships that I didn't think I would get when I'm here.

After the Vietnam War in 1975, my grandparents tried to leave Vietnam because they wanted freedom for themselves. They tried to get on a boat to get over here to America and failed three times. My mom told me that on the third try, the mafia came and took all their money away from them. And then, the neighbors would come rob their house, so when they got back to their house, there was nothing there. Plus, my grandfather went to jail for trying to leave the country. My mom and grandmother had to do all the work so they could get money to bail my grandfather out of jail.

My grandfather's sister took them to the US finally, but my mom had to wait because she was over twenty-one. After I was born, we had to wait twelve years to come here for a big reunion, so we could meet everybody that came over here.

I was actually in third grade when my mother said that we were going to come to the US. I got excited. I was the first person who saw the email that said we got a visa. I got excited! Everybody was. My parents gave up a lot of things for us to be able to come over here.

We had to wait three more years until we were actually going to the US. I still remember the day my mom said that we were going to go to the airport the next week. The last day of school that I went to, I sat there and my tears just came out. I was asked if I was okay and said, "yes," but I didn't know. I felt like I was about to leave my stuff over there: my coach, my friends, all the good things.

I still remember the time before we got into the plane. It was a horrible experience for me. We didn't speak English, except my mom, who spoke a little bit. She couldn't speak well though because she got sick with a cold. It was difficult just to get the papers set up and on the plane. My mom was crying; the tears just came out. On the inside, I wanted to, but I couldn't. I walked to the airport, turned my back, and kept going.

When we got to Atlanta, there was a reunion. I got to see my grandparents, my cousins, my aunt, and my uncle, and we started hugging each other. My aunt was crying because she hadn't seen her sister for five years. I hadn't seen them for six or seven years and my grandparents for eight years.

After we got into the car, I saw the cars and houses, and they were so nice. I remember thinking I was happy now and I had a better life. The first day was okay. I slept all during the first week because of the time change. The first month after that was really hard for me because everything returned back to normal for my family. My aunt's family had to go back to where they lived, and my grandparents had to go back to work, so the house was empty. We didn't know anything. We didn't know where to go, how to speak the language well, or how to drive. It was just like we were stuck.

Getting unstuck took getting me into school. The first day of school, I still remember to this day. They put me in a class full of students, gave me the test, and told me to take it. After that, I put my head down and started crying like a baby. I felt like everything was wrong, and I just gave up on that day. From that point, I didn't like school anymore. Time kept going on though, so I had to get back up on it. I joined football, wrestling, and soccer, and it helped me get unstuck.

I went to Sequoyah Middle School at the end of sixth grade. It was funny because I spoke English to other people and they laughed at me. They laughed at my accent. I was confused and thought, "Why do they have to laugh at me?" Just because we came from another country didn't mean they had to laugh at me.

I was quiet at first, but around friends I talked a lot. It took a while to make friends, but I made them because I was good at math and through the football team. Those friendships didn't last that long though because they had my back sometimes but not all the time. When I came to Cross Keys, I met more friends. It's really good to have friends that are beside you every time you're down because they help you up.

There was a lot that my family gave up to come to the US. My parents gave up everything for us because they lived in Vietnam for forty years. I gave up a lot, too: my school, my friendships, my coach, and even the environment around me. But I can't give up. Sadness makes me stronger than ever.

I could say that I'm happy now though. My life is so great now that I learned how to be a good guy. I got to know a lot of other people who helped me out. But there's always a good side and a bad side. A good side is that I get an education and the reunion of my family. The bad side is that I miss the feeling of my family eating together. For dinner in Vietnam, we would all eat together, but it's not the same over here. I feel like we're disconnected. My dad has to wake up at 3:00 in the morning and work until 3:00 or 5:00 in the afternoon. My mom has to work too starting at like 9:00, so I don't see her that much. For me, surviving over here is like being independent. You have to do it by yourself.

For me, the American Dream is first about education, and second about more income. People come here for education to get more jobs and more money to help their family. I am able to study over here, and that's good for me. I have the opportunity to figure out my future instead of using all of my time to study. I can say that I am a lucky person.

I want to go to college. I have two things in mind right now. First, I want to be a businessman so I can help my family. I like living here, but I want to work in my country. I want to do international marketing because I miss and love my country. My uncle is a businessman. He takes care of his family well, so I want to be like him. Secondly, I want to be a counselor because I don't want other students to go through what I have been through.

VIDEO LINKS

greencardvoices.org/speakers/hau-phuong-vo

Banjul,
The Gambia

Kumba Njie

Born: Atlanta, GA   **Raised:** Banjul, The Gambia
Current City: Atlanta, GA

> "I REMEMBER MY MOM USED TO SEND US MONEY IN AFRICA, AND SO I THOUGHT THAT SHE WAS DOING REALLY WELL, BUT WHEN I CAME TO AMERICA, I REALIZED THAT SHE WAS ACTUALLY STRUGGLING."

I was lucky enough to be born in America, but when I was really young I was sent to West Africa. I was raised in Gambia. I lived there with my grandparents, my two other sisters, and my aunt. Life there was very simple and nice. It was just big and warm, and you were never alone. It was wonderful there. The reason why I love it so much there, even though it was crazy and underdeveloped, was because we had a wonderful family unit. I loved my grandparents. I was sent there when I was a couple months old, so I didn't really know my parents. Even today, I think I'm learning more and more about them. I kind of grew up as having my grandparents be like my parents. My grandparents were wonderful. They were fun. And so were my sisters. I grew up with my two older sisters. Thank God they were too busy fighting with each other, so I got to be friends with them. I had a lot of friends there. It wasn't the ideal place to develop and grow into somebody that's going to be successful. That's why I came here.

My mom wanted me to come here, so she had her two daughters (my two older sisters) in Africa, and then she basically came here for, I believe, the same thing that she brought us here for: for a better life, better opportunities. She came alone, and I believe my dad followed right behind. They had me and my younger sister here. I think that she sent us back over to Gambia because, over here, everything is a lot more expensive and difficult. So she sent us back to live with our grandparents—that way, she could provide for us and when we were ready, we could come back. I remember my mom used to send us money in Africa, and so I thought that she was doing really well. But when I came to America, I realized that she was actually struggling.

The education there—it's behind. I basically got good grades there, and I believe that's one of the reasons they wanted to bring me back. Still

9

today, the education there affects me. I still mess up my "hes" and "shes", but my writing is improving. I didn't like the fact that in the schools, they used to beat you, but when you don't know anything else, it's just like, this is the situation, and you're okay with it. Overall, I didn't see it as something bad. I had a lot of fun there. I had a lot of friends, and life was great. We celebrated holidays there, and my family just made it amazing.

I remember we celebrated Tabaski and Ramadan. Those were like Christmas there. We used to get dressed very nice then have parties at night. We'd go to the mosque, and we'd pray. It was all very fun and exciting. I remember we didn't have school on those days. I remember that our other family members that didn't live with us used to come to our house, and we'd have this big party. I enjoyed those holidays.

When I found out I was coming to America, it wasn't really this, "Sit down, we have to tell you something important." It was like I kind of knew because they were talking about it. I don't think I would've had a say in whether or not I was going. I don't think that was my choice. I wouldn't blame them because I was like nine or ten. I would've probably said that I wanted to stay there. I kind of just found out. It was lurking around the house. It was just like, "Okay well she's going. She already knows." When the day came, my grandmother helped me pack my bag.

I remember I packed my clothes. I had this pearl necklace that I was wearing, my hair was braided, and I brought the one Cinderella book I had. Me and my two aunts got in the car, and we had to cross the river. So we drove all the way to where the ferry was, then our car had to go on the ferry. It was scary because we were the first, and they had one chain that was keeping the cars from falling off the boat. They were trying to get us to push forward. We said, "We don't want to fall over," but they said, "Keep going." Luckily the rules over there were very loose on seat belts. I remember I was sitting on one of my aunts, and my other auntie was holding my little sister.

After we crossed the ferry, it was just more driving. We had a lot of stops on the road with the police. Security was heavy there. We drove to the airport until late at night. It was very nice there. It was bright and shiny. There were nice pictures. Of course, it was a bit small. I remember that I went to the bathroom and that when I came back it was time to go. My sister was leaving, and the airplane attendant or some lady was like, "It's time to go. Come on. Come on." We got on the plane, so I never got to say goodbye to my two aunts officially.

I believe it was a long flight, ten to fourteen hours. We watched *Toy Story*. We watched it multiple times because we were just so happy. I believe that's the first kid cartoon we ever watched. I think it was overnight because they served us breakfast, but at that time, the food tasted very weird. I remember that when the man came around he was probably expecting me to be say, "I want juice," but I was like "I want tea." He started to look at me a little bit like I was crazy.

We stopped in New York, and that's where our mom was waiting for us. She was very excited. She sent me when I was so young, so it was like I was seeing her for the first time. For a second, she felt a bit like a stranger, but it was nice. We got in a car, and we went to stay with my mom's close friend for a couple of days. Then after that, we got on another plane, but that one brought us here to Atlanta. When we got here, we went to visit my other aunt, and that's where we stayed for a couple weeks.

When I first got here, it was very different. There were so many different people. I went from seeing everybody with the same skin color—maybe every now and then I'd see somebody that's light-skinned—to seeing so many different colors and so many different cultures everywhere. It was wonderful, but it was different. There were so many people and so many different foods and different smells and big cars, and even at that time, the roads seemed nice. You didn't see trash. In Gambia, there was always trash on the roads. I remember I was walking through New York when we were going to our apartment, some kids were just having a normal American drama situation and I was just like, "That's so different." I remember for some reason me and my sister used to fight over who got to push the shopping cart or who got to push the elevator button.

At first, I lived with my aunt and her husband for a little bit. It was a change, definitely, because I went from a big family (every day there was noise everywhere) to it being small and quiet and having to learn all the new "dos and don'ts."

Going to school was different too. The whole situation was just a crazy time to adapt. Kids there were mean, but, as you learn afterwards, kids are just naturally like that. When you are in an environment where everybody is the same kind of color as you, it's easier. So making friends was easier in Gambia. Also, I felt as if I went from being a top student to all the way down. It was kind of crazy because I was like, "What is the teacher talking about?" I remember some of my teachers in Africa spoke English, but they transitioned from English to Wolof, so it was very different to have these teachers who never spoke the language I was speaking. It was kind of like they threw you in the pool.

I was definitely failing. I do not want to relive the whole educational part when I first got here because I just didn't like it. It just didn't fit me. I felt like I had to adapt, and it took me a long time. Luckily, I was able to catch up fast, but it was difficult when I first got here. It's still difficult sometimes.

My life over here is—it's different. It's definitely not like when I was back there. I know that here it's a lot more challenging and it's a lot more difficult, and it basically pushes me to the limit. I think even though it does that, it's setting you up for a better future and a good life. When I got here, things like music attracted me very much. Now I can't go a day without listening to music.

I also work after school at Taco Bell, and it's very fun there. It's a very small store, and it's like you know everyone over there and everyone knows you. So it's very nice and comfortable. I also have multiple club activities that I do, which makes my schedule busier, but you have to prepare and be ready for a higher education. I work hard at school and study, and it's just to make sure I have my dream job. I think it's probably just because I want to be my own boss. In a way, that's kind of why I appreciate coming back here. It's because I don't think I would have realized this when I was in Gambia. I would have probably chosen to do something basic, but here, the fact that I want to aim so high is . . . it's wonderful. Even though there were some bumps in the road at the beginning, I feel like I'm definitely doing better and I'm growing out of it. But it is still difficult at times.

The clubs that I participate in are very wonderful, and they help me blend better into the environment and help me adapt. I am part of the debate club, psychology club, and student council. I'm also part of a the entrepreneur clubs, and I just joined the National Honors Society for Social Studies. These clubs are very close to me. I feel very attached to them. Maybe it's because I feel as if they set me on a good path. I want to be somebody who creates businesses and helps the economy grow. I want to be a public figure. and I want to be a very successful entrepreneur.

I want to be a public figure because I want to be able to help people and make a difference for others in situations like mine. I was lucky that I was able to get on a plane and come here, but that's not how it is for everyone, and I feel for them. When I see stuff on the news about people dying at the borders, I can understand their struggle. What seems to us like everyday privilege, people from other countries are dying for. People see a lot of people coming to our borders but don't take the time to learn why they are coming.

I pay attention to politics. It's important to me to pay attention and be aware. Sometimes people don't pay attention to the politicians and the government and how bad things are around the world, even though it's right in front of our faces. I don't want to be blind to what is going on around me. I feel like I grew up fast, but I had to. I think it's important for all people my age to pay attention to what's going on around us because it will prep us for making the right decisions when it comes time to vote. There are some things like this that they should teach in high school that are important for us to learn. If we are more prepared, it could save us from a lot of negative situations.

The American Dream to me is basically the opportunity to have a new start or to get a better opportunity, and just to have a better life. There are many, many, many places around the world where you don't get certain opportunities because of certain restrictions and wars. Here you're given the opportunity, and that's what everybody wants. That's why so many people are flooding to our door, trying to get a better life. So for me, the American Dream is hope. Because the reason why so many people are coming here is because they hope for a new life—a better life—because they don't want to suffer anymore. To me, that's what the American Dream is.

VIDEO LINKS

greencardvoices.org/speakers/kumba-njie

Guadalupe,
Mexico

Mario

From: Guadalupe, Mexico
Current City: Atlanta, GA

"I BELIEVE THAT THE AMERICAN DREAM IS TO PURSUE YOUR PASSION IN THE UNITED STATES WITHOUT FEARING ANY DISCRIMINATION OR ANY OBSTACLES IN TERMS OF PERSONAL APPEARANCES AND BASICALLY OVERALL DISCRIMINATION."

I was born in Guadalupe, Zacatecas, Mexico. I grew up in what we call La Blanca, Zacatecas, Mexico, but its official name is General Pánfilo Natera, Zacatecas, Mexico. I honestly don't remember much from my time in Mexico because I was there for a short amount of time. But the few memories that I do have are all the memories that I have of my childhood.

I came to the United States when I was about six months old for the first time. Then, because of some complications, me and my mom had to return back to Mexico, and we lived with my grandparents. In the house, there were my grandparents, my mom, me (I was the only grandkid), her two sisters and her brother—so, my two aunts and my uncle. I remember it was very desert-like there. Not much vegetation—I actually don't remember any grass—except a couple of trees. And, I remember walking, mostly alone or accompanied by my grandfather, who was the music teacher, to school because there was no public transportation to my preschool. There were just dirt roads all the way there and back. My mom helped tend to two stores. One was a candy store, which was across from a medical store—they sold herbal medicines. Whenever I was done with school, I would go help her out with the candy store. We would spend the day like that and then come back to my grandparents' house. As a kid, I was very antisocial, you could say. I didn't have many friends, maybe one or two. We played occasionally, but most of my time, I spent in the backyard playing with nature, either rock collecting or observing scorpions.

I honestly didn't know that I had come to the United States before this time. Like I said, all of my memories of my childhood were in Mexico so I actually thought I was raised in Mexico. However, because of a couple of pictures that were sent from Mexico marking the tenth year anniversary of our departure and the whole DACA process I uncovered my real childhood, which consisted of me coming to the United States when I was six months old and staying until I was about three years. I didn't know that until I saw pictures of myself on a beach in

15

Panama City Beach and standing in snow in Detroit. I never knew I had visited those places until seeing those photos, which ended up being backed up with the acquaintance of my father.

Then, when I was three years old, still in the United States, my father told us that he couldn't be a part of my family anymore because he wanted a different life for himself. He told my mom to find her own life. My mom was devastated because of that. So, we sought refuge back in Mexico at her parents' house—without those pictures I might have never known this because I don't recall anything that happened prior to, and including, my father leaving us. So I grew up thinking that I never had a father, and that's why, I guess, it hurts more.

When I was around five years old, a bit after my birthday, he came to Mexico and basically told our little town his personal reason for leaving. My mom felt that I would be persecuted, in a way, because I was the target, and she didn't want that to get in the way of my life. So we came to the United States to escape that persecution. We came here for the second time in June when I was about to turn six, and we lived with my mom's distant aunt for a couple months until my mom found a job and we were relatively stable.

I actually remember my first week in the US. We stopped in some hotel in Texas. I remember having to walk down the streets to get something to eat because we didn't have anything. There was a taquería down the street, and we were like, "Tacos, somewhat a part of our home," so that's why we ate there; however, it was pretty bad. I had a very bad experience there—it was trash compared to our home.

So, our first week was not the best. From Texas, we came to Georgia by train. I remember waking up really early and packing only one book bag; mine was full of clothes and memorabilia (pictures of family and CDs from our country). However, due to the limitations, a lot of important or cherished items were lost. When we came to Georgia, we settled in with my mom's aunt, and then we moved to an apartment. My first school was in Fulton County; I was in first grade. I remember I was one of only two Hispanics in the entire school. Everybody was mostly White, and they did not like me very much because of my differences. They would bully me, and I only had one friend again—he was Black. I had never been social, so it didn't bother me. But, the biggest bully was the only other Hispanic boy, which hurt more, making me feel shamed by a fellow Hispanic.

I was a nerdy kid. I had a deep passion for math and science. Having this passion made the transition easier. Coming to the United States, math was the one subject that stayed constant, and I didn't have to learn new words because it's basically the same thing. Math and science were really important throughout my life, and with that, I was able to adapt quickly. I set my future and my aspirations within the STEM department because I found a passion with using science and mathematics for programming and computer science. I plan to venture out into higher education pursuing a major in computer science.

After the first semester in the all-White school, we moved to Atlanta where I've stayed for the past ten years. Moving here, I went to the school that was just down the street, Woodward Elementary, and back in the day, it was mostly Hispanic so it wasn't much of a difference. Well, it was different coming from the all-White school to an all-Hispanic school, but I felt more accepted in my community. Moving from there to Sequoyah Middle School, same thing—it was all Hispanic. Then, Cross Keys is still the same; it's been mostly Hispanic so that might have some effect on me going back into an all-White college.

Once I graduate from college, I plan to get an internship to get some experience within computer science, and I plan to start my own business in the video game industry. After I become successful, I will return back to my community and give back to the people and organizations who have helped me. I also plan to create scholarships and opportunities that I couldn't get because of my status as a DACA student. A lot of the good scholarships that are out there, I'm not eligible for. So I want to open that up to more generations with similar struggles.

I believe that the American Dream is to pursue your passion in the United States without fearing any discrimination or any obstacles in terms of personal appearances and basically overall discrimination. I think the American Dream is succeeding and going further, beyond what you would normally have and pursuing a better life for you and your family without prejudices because of your parents or your background.

If I didn't come to the United States, I would probably be a part of some drug cartel or be dead already. I don't know. With the current situation in Mexico, it's very dangerous to be over there, and hearing conversations from my grandmother and mom, most of the people that I grew up with in my preschool have already dropped out of school when they were in sixth grade and they have kids. They're not doing well, so I probably wouldn't have been doing well either if I had stayed behind.

VIDEO LINKS

greencardvoices.org/speakers/mario

Tlangpi,
Myanmar

Nu Nu

From: Tlangpi, Chin State, Myanmar
Current City: Atlanta, GA

"ON JANUARY 27TH, 2015, MY UNCLE GOT A PHONE CALL FOR US TO INTERVIEW AT THE EMBASSY TO GO TO THE USA. HE WAS SO HAPPY. HE WAS JUMPING!"

My name is Nu Nu; I was born in Myanmar Chin State, Tlangpi. When I lived in my country, I lived with my grandparents because of family problems. When I lived in my country, I went to school from first grade through third. My grandparents could not really work hard, so we did not have money to pay the fee, so I stopped going to school, and I helped my grandparents make farm. We carried buckets of water and cooked and cleaned. My life in my country was hard.

My uncle worked as a missionary. The Myanmar people did not want my uncle to tell about God. "If you come in my country, we will kill you," they said. My uncle did not listen to them. He kept telling about God. The Myanmar people reported my uncle to the army. The army came in his house, and they burnt it. My uncle did not care, and he talked about God and Christians. They said again, "We are going to kill you," and they came. My uncle's friend came and told my uncle, "You are not safe in here anymore so go run away in India," and my uncle was scared. He ran away to India. After he was in India for a while, my grandparents sent me and my sister, Te Te, with my uncle to India when I was ten.

In India I lived in a house. This was hard because it was only one room and no kitchen. We did not have a bed. My parents died when I was young, and my uncle adopted me and my sister. I lived with my uncle, auntie, Te Te, and two girl cousins. In India I went to school. I continued to fourth grade. And after fourth grade, I could not continue because we did not have money to pay the fee. My uncle has an eye problem, and he cannot really work hard. So I did not start school with my sister. My auntie is a tailor and can sew clothes. When we got the money, we bought food. We did not have a lot of stuff. At night in India, at the market, the people left food. We went and

19

we took and we ate what was left. After two years we went to a refugee school. In India I played volleyball with my friends for fun. It is so different in India than in America. Life in India was so hard. So now here is really cool. I like it.

On January 27th, 2015, my uncle got a phone call for us to interview at the embassy to go to the USA. He was so happy. He was jumping! My uncle told us, "We are going to the USA interview," and we were so excited. It was amazing! We knew if we could go to the USA, we could get a better future and go to school. Before we came to the USA, we had four interviews that were resettlement, IOM, embassy, and medical check-up. We all had to go to them.

So in June we came to the United States in an airplane. It was so difficult. We did not know how to order food because we had not gone out to a restaurant before, and we did not speak English. I was scared of the airplane bathroom, and I had not gone in an airplane before. It was so difficult in an airplane. We first arrived in London, and then flew to Chicago, and then to Atlanta.

When we first arrived in Atlanta, we stayed in a hotel. We stayed three days, and after three days, we went to our house. When I saw my house for the first time, I said, "I do not believe this!" We all have our own room now. It is much bigger than our house in India. We have a big kitchen and big bedrooms and big restrooms. We live by a park, and because there are a lot of trees, I call it "the forest in Atlanta." The house was good, but there were no Burmese people, no friends, and that was so difficult for me. My family did not go outside because we did not have friends, and we were so bored. White people came to the park and I wanted to talk to them, but I did not know English. It was all English-speaking people. We just stayed home, and at night we did not sleep because it was so different. In the morning we slept. In Atlanta at our house, we go to the market to get food. We have more food options than we did in India. We buy the food we want. When we want it, we buy the food and we eat it. We buy a lot of vegetables, chicken, and beef. My favorite food to get at the market is Takis.

We did not go to school at first. On my first day of school, I was really nervous because my English was so broken. My first day of school was good, but I did not have any friends. I sat alone and ate alone. I liked all of my teachers. The teachers were nice. They told the other students that I am new to school and to be my friend. After four days, I got friends. I have a best friend now too.

My favorite subjects at school are English and social studies. I want to be a lawyer. I want to be the best lawyer. When I finish high school and college, I will go back to my country to help my people and my village in Myanmar. If I cannot be a lawyer, I want to be a teacher and teach people in Myanmar how to speak English. Because we are moving to South Carolina soon for my uncle to be a pastor at a church there, I do not know where I will go to college or high school.

I am on the JV soccer team for Clarkston High School. I do not give up. I just play. During the week I go to soccer practice, take care of my cousins (they are eight, five, and one), do my homework, help clean the house, and watch videos on YouTube. And on the weekend, I go to church. I like to sing at church. Sometimes they say, "You are going to sing today," so I sing for them. I like to sing, and I want to be a singer. My favorite band is Hillsong.

Now my life is so good. Life was so different before the USA, and now I can go to school. I can get what I want for lunch here. What I want to do, I can do here. If I had stayed in Myanmar, my life would be different because I could not go to school. I would have to help my grandparents on the farm. Maybe the army would kill us. Maybe I would die if I stayed in my village. It's different. My grandparents are still in our village, and I talk to them sometimes. When I talk to them, my grandmother says to me, "We do not need to forget about our past. Our past can help us to get better." My uncle had an eye operation, and his eye problems are better now. Some of my friends from India still live there and some of them live in Australia now. I hear from them on Facebook sometimes.

VIDEO LINKS

greencardvoices.org/speakers/nu-nu

Conakry, Guinea

Abdoulaye Diallo

From: Conakry, Guinea
Current City: Atlanta, GA

> "IN SENEGAL I WAS LOST FOR FOUR YEARS. I LIVED BY MYSELF IN THE STREET. LIFE IN THE STREET WAS FULL OF TROUBLE."

I was born in Guinea. In Guinea, it was fun and cool going to school with my friends and playing. After school, I would go play soccer, stay with my friend, and make tea. When it was the right time, we would go steal mangos. We had little bags to put the mangos in. We would go to my house and say, "Look how much we got." Whoever had less than five mangos we wouldn't follow them anymore to try to steal their mangos. We didn't have enough money to buy a soccer ball, so we had to go sell the mangos to people. When we got the money, we went and bought a ball to play soccer, tea, and sugar.

My dad came to the United States before I was born. He stayed there but came to Guinea for a while, then came and went back a lot. One day in 2003, he decided to bring us here. He sent the papers and the visa. My mom put the papers and passports under the bed. We had some rats in the house, and they ate all the papers and passports. Then we had to wait until 2016 to come to the US.

My dad told me and my brother to go to Senegal to learn Arabic and so we went there. My dad said if we didn't go there, he wouldn't bring us to the United States. So, we decided to go there and learn for a while. We left my family in Guinea and went to Senegal. It was nice for the first month, but after that, it wasn't nice. A lot of people got sick.

We stayed there for a while. After the first month, our teacher had another teacher teach us Arabic. That teacher was so mean to us because we didn't know how to read, but he tried to force us to read real quick. He knew if we read real quick my dad would send money to him. If we worked, they had to feed us, but if we didn't work, they didn't have to feed us. If we wanted dinner, we had to go at 12:00 pm to get dinner and go beg for money from people. If people gave us money, we couldn't take the money. We had to give the money to the teacher. The teacher took the money and used it to buy gas or food for his family. So we stayed there. The restroom was terrible and had little bugs all in it. A lot of people came in there. People traveling all around came in our restroom. It was so nasty there.

In Senegal, I was lost for four years. I lived by myself in the street. Life in the street was full of trouble. When we went to Senegal to learn, I didn't like it there. It was nasty, and I told my mom I didn't want to stay there. The teachers said, "You have to stay here. Don't call your mom." When I asked my teacher for permission to call my mom, he said, "If you call your mom, I'm going to beat you up." I said, "Alright, alright." Then he said, "In the morning, you will be beat with a belt 5,000 times." I thought, "Oh wow, I don't want to get beat," and then I ran. I went to the bus station where they have a lot of buses. People travel all around the country by bus. They go to Guinea, Gambia, Mali, and other countries in Africa. I saw a person who owned a bus; he was the bus driver. I said, "I want to work here with you. Can you let me on your bus to sleep there?" He said, "Well, you have to work but we don't pay you. You are just working for us. We don't have to pay you, but we have to give you food and a place to stay, we don't buy clothes for you, just food." I said, "Oh, alright, I'm cool with that." I started working there, going to places like Tambacounda, and working hard. It was horrible there. Then one day they took me to a different place that I didn't know, and they just left me there. I was going to the restroom, and when I came back, I couldn't find the bus. The bus was gone. They left me there. I said, "What the heck?" I was wondering where I would live now.

The teacher called my mom and said, "We haven't seen your son here for two weeks." My mom started wondering, "Where is my son?" She started crying and came to Senegal to look for me. I didn't know my mom was there. If I knew, I would have gone back to meet her to take me back to Guinea. I was sleeping on the street, begging for money. It was horrible. I got in fights with a lot of little kids who lived on the street too. If I got money, the little kids would say, "Give me your money or I'm going to get you killed. I'm going to kick you." I said "No." Sometimes, if the kid was bigger than me, I would give my money to them because I didn't want to fight. I didn't want to get hit. One day I didn't eat food at all. I just ate candy that some people gave me. I didn't know where I was going to sleep when I was sleeping on the street.

At a restaurant, I met a guy who spoke the same language as me. He said, "Where you come from?" I said, "I come from Guinea." He said, "Oh, me too. I come from Guinea too." That was when I realized he was my best friend when I was young in Guinea. He said, "Why you look like this? You don't have nice clothes, no?" I said, "I'm lost. I don't know where to go. Can you help me?" He said, "Yes, of course. Come on." Then he led me into the restaurant and said, "What you need? You have to take a shower?" I said, "Yes, of course." He gave me one coin to go take a shower in the bathroom. You have to pay there in the bathhouse if you are going to take a shower. He let me take a shower, and when I came back, he said, "What you need? You need food? I got a little bread here if you want some." He gave me the bread, and I ate it all. I was sitting there the next day, and he brought me rice to eat. Then two guys came and said, "Hey boy, give me your food or I'm going to kick you." I said, "No, I can't give you my food, but if you want, you can come sit with me. We can eat together, but you don't have to take my food and go." They said they were going to beat me up if I did not give them my food. I said, "No," then they punched me in the face, and I fell down. They took my food and left. I couldn't say anything. If I said something or screamed, they would come back and beat me. I sat and looked at them as they ate all my food.

I went to work, and I saw an old man who had a lot of big bags. I said, "Can I help you?" He said, "Yes, of course." I took his bags to another place, and he paid me five dollars. A group of boys were following me and said, "Give me your money." I ran and jumped on a slow-moving train before they could catch me. I jumped off the train to the other side of the tracks and left them. They were waiting for the train to pass so they could come get my money, but by the time the train passed, I was gone.

When I went to the restaurant, my friend said, "Hey, you don't have to be scared. You have to be strong and fight back." I said, "No, I don't want to." He said, "If you are scared, they are going to come beat you up every day and take your clothes and money. If you are not scared, they're going to leave you alone." The next day, the same group of boys, about five boys, came and said, "Hey boy, give me your shoes. Give me your shirt." I said, "No, I'm not giving you anything." My friend was standing there and said, "Hey boy, don't be scared, fight back." I started fighting back and punched one of the guys. He fell down, and I punched them more. They all ran. The guy was going to bring another group of people to fight back because my friend was teaching me how to fight. They tried to fight my friend. My friend brought a knife from the restaurant. He told them, "If you come here, I'm going to kill you." After that day, they never came back. They all ran away.

I worked for the restaurant for a while, and they didn't pay me anything. It was okay because I was getting food, I was getting to take showers, I got shoes and all that stuff. I slept in the restaurant and cleaned the floors. They let me sleep there because if I slept outside, a lot of people would come take my clothes off and take my shoes and run or take my money. Then I would have to sleep on the ground, but I wouldn't have anything to cover myself. I would sleep on the ground with nothing to sleep on. All night, there are bugs, some dogs bark at you. You would have to throw something at them because if not, they were going to bite you. You had to beat them, so they would run away from where you were sleeping on the street.

For three years, I was on the street and working hard. If I saw some people that had big bags they could not lift by themselves, I would say, "Can I help you?" If they said yes, I would help. When I brought the bags to another place, they paid me like five bucks. I kept my money and went to the store and bought some clothes and shoes. I didn't have to buy something for my mom because I didn't know where they lived.

One day I saw a guy who knew me from the school and knew where I came from. He said, "You don't have to work. Your mom is wondering where you are." He said my mom was in Dakar. I said, "No, that is not true. You want to take me back there, and they will beat me. I'm not going back there." He said, "Okay, let's stay here. I'm going to call your mom and tell her I found you." He took the phone and called my teacher. He said, "We found Abdoulaye here. He is here with me." My teacher said, "Hold him! Hold him hard. Don't let him go!" I said, "Don't hold me, or I'm going to punch you. I'm not running. If my mom comes, I'm going to stay here, but if the teacher comes, I'm going to run."

My brother told me when they first saw me, they were a little far away and my head was turned. I had a lot of hair. My little brother said, "Oh, that is Abdoulaye right there." My mom said, "No, that is not my son. What the . . . that is not my son." My brother said, "Yes, of course, that is Abdoulaye! Look! Look very closely." Then they came closer. My mom was looking and said, "No, that is not my son. He has more hair than I remember. Why would he look like that? No, that is not my son." My brother said, "Yes." My mom started crying and held me, hugging and crying.

Then they took me to the house in Senegal. When I got to the house, they asked me, "What do you want? I'm going to buy it for you." I said, "No, I don't want anything. I am happy just to see you." They said, "Me too. Why did you run? You made us sad." When I was lost, my mom was thinking about me: where I was, how I was doing. When I got back to the home, my mom said, "When you take a shower, I'm going to go take you to get your hair cut." I said, "Okay." They took me there. When I came back, they gave me some food to eat and had me sleep and stay with my family.

My teacher called, and my mom told him they found me. He said, "Oh, you found Abdoulaye. Just bring him here. We want to see him." He said they were not going to beat me, that they wanted me to come back. I never saw the teacher again. Then my mom brought me to the embassy. The embassy was so happy to see me. They said, "We called you to come to the US, but we didn't see you. You were lost." They asked me why. I told them what it was like at the school, how terrible it was, and that I could not stay there, so I tried to run and escape. I stayed for one more year in Senegal, and then they called me to come to the US. When I received my passport to come to the United States, my mom said, "Don't stay here. Go real quick before the passport expires." I said, "I want to go back to Guinea, and visit my family." She said, "No, you have to go right now from Senegal. You take a plane and go." I said, "Alright, I'll go back to Guinea when I graduate." She said, "Alright, no problem."

When we went to the airport, it was very cold, and my family was there waiting with me before it was time to get on the plane. I was getting upset with my family, who was too cold. My mom went inside to check in for the flight. When she came out, I had to go inside the plane. My family could not come into the airport with me because they had a lot of security. So they stayed there. My family got cold waiting for me to go. They were going to go back to the house, and I said, "Just go to the house because outside is too cold. You cannot stay here. You have to go." They said, "No, we decided to wait. We are going to wait for you. When you go, we are going to go."

When me and my mom went inside the airport, the police standing there said, "What are you doing here with your son?" She said, "I'm showing him where the airplane is because he doesn't know." The police said, "You can't come here. You have to show me your ID." Another good police guy came and said, "Let them in. This is a little kid. She just has to show him where the airplane is, where you have to go and sign all the papers, and where you have to put your book bag on the machine that takes it to the plane." When I was walking up to the airplane, my mom just looked at me and started crying. She said, "Goodbye. I'm so happy." When I was going up the stairs, my mom could not go with me. I said, "Mom, come with me. Come." But my mom could not come because she didn't have the papers. I said, "Come with me. Nobody's here. Come." She said, "No, just go." She was crying, and I was crying too. When I got on the airplane and left my mom, I was scared. I didn't know anybody.

When I sat on the airplane and it started to fly for a while, they served people food and I wanted to go to the restroom to brush my teeth. I didn't know how to use the restroom. It was my first time on the airplane. I turned on the faucet, and water sprayed all over me. I couldn't turn it off. I ran out and the worker said, "What you need?" I said, "I need to brush my teeth." He showed me how to turn it on without all the water spraying. I didn't know how to open the door when I was inside. I just knocked for someone to open the door because if you enter, the doors were going to lock.

I went from Senegal to Paris, and the airplane sat there, waiting for people to get in and fly straight to America. When the plane was in Paris, I looked, and I thought it was America. I asked someone, "Where is it here?" He said, "Here is Paris." I said, "Oh no, how? I don't want to go to Paris. I want to go to USA. Where can I find the airplane to go straight to US?" He took me to the office desk and the people knew where I was going because they saw my American passport. When I showed my passport to the lady, she said, "I know where you're going. Your name is on the list." Then she took me straight to the airplane and asked me, "What you need? Do you need food?" I said, "No," because I was nervous. I wanted to eat, but I was nervous and decided to sit and wait. When I saw my dad and my sister, then I was going to eat.

I came here by myself. All the English signs in the airport were terrible to me because I didn't know how to read English. I asked someone, "What is this? Where is the airplane?" They said, "Excuse me, I have to go." I asked some people, they said, "No, I don't know where you are going." I just sat on the chair looking at the letters on the signs, and then I realized I have to translate, and I wrote in French and translated.

When I arrived, I saw my sister waiting for me. My family all jumped on me. I was surprised. I didn't know that they were there because I didn't have a cell phone on me. Before that, my cell phone was not working on the airplane because the airplane mode doesn't work. My dad was waiting for me in the parking lot, and he took me to the house. I saw all the big woods, and I thought, "What the heck? This is America? I know America is full of the tallest buildings, I know America is that." When I saw the woods, I said, "This is not America." I was confused. My dad said, "Yea it is! Here is Atlanta. You have to go downtown before you see all the nice buildings."

My first friends at school were Kennedy—he's my best friend—and one girl, Kin, who was so fun. Kennedy was so cool. He came to my apartment, played with me, and Kin was cool too. When she sat in class, she would talk to me. I didn't understand what she was talking about. She speaks Chinese, so I didn't know what she was saying. She spoke better English than me. I just knew, "How are you? How you doing? Where you going? Where you want to eat?" She turned to me and said, "Do you want to come with me to the lunch?" I didn't know what she said. I just sat on the chair. She taught me how to be brave and speak out. She said, "You have to say something." She took me by my hand and said, "Let's go. Don't be scared. Let's go to the lunch." I saw a lot of people at the lunch sitting. When I came in, people looked at me. I said, "I don't want to eat." I went to the restroom and sat on the toilet. When the bell rang, I went to class.

Coming to America, it was hard to have to leave my family and leave my friends. All my friends said, "When you coming back? We miss you. Come join us playing. We are so fun. Here is cool." I said, "Alright, I will come back when I am done with school." But they miss me a lot. My grandma said, "Oh wow, you have to come here now. You have been in America for a while." I said, "Nah, I have just been here two years. You miss me?" She said, "Yeah." They want me to go back. I said, "Alright, I will."

I want to be in the US for a while and understand English, how to speak well, and how to write and read real quick. I want to be a music singer and an artist. I'm working on my music. I want to be a music producer. In Guinea, if I were a singer there, they would have to kick me out of the house. People would say, "You can't stay here . . . you are not a good person . . . you want to be a criminal," all that stuff. You know Guinea is a Muslim country. You can't do what you want. You have to follow the rules. So, I decided to write and wait for when I live by myself and have my own house and start doing my thing. I write my own hip-hop lyrics. I like writing hip-hop. I like listening to Future, Desiigner, and all those famous music rappers. I also want to make my story into a movie.

VIDEO LINKS

greencardvoices.org/speakers/abdoulaye-diallo

Rajshahi,
Bangladesh

HM Sakib

From: Rajshahi, Bangladesh
Current City: Atlanta, GA

> "I JUST WANT TO HELP THE WORLD BECOME A BETTER PLACE. BUT IT'S FRUSTRATING THAT I CAN'T DO IT ALL MYSELF. I NEED MORE. WE NEED EVERYONE TO COMMIT TO IT."

I'm from Rajshahi. There are not a lot of people from Rajshahi. I think I'm the only one around here. Everybody here is from Sylhet, and they have their own dialect. The way they speak Bengali is not the same way as mine. So, I don't know what they're saying. Mine is more like the proper way to speak it. Theirs is more like slang; it makes no sense to me. I'm just teasing of course. Sylhetis are cool.

I also learned how to read Arabic because I am Muslim. Even though I learned how to read it, I don't know what it says. But, I can read it. That's about it.

I'm going to start with the good things about Bangladesh. I'm seventeen now, and I'm from Rajshahi, Bangladesh. It's a small town. People know their neighbors; we know who's who. We know everybody's business. We know what's going on. Word gets out fast. It's a pretty cool neighborhood. When I was a kid there, all my childhood friends were there, too. I would go play in this big field right behind my house. My dad owned a lot of the land there, including the field. We would go there and play every afternoon. It was fun.

Most of my family lived in Rajshahi, too, from both my mom's side and my dad's side. I would take slow walks to my grandma's house sometimes. My mom said it was five minutes away walking. Grandma had a little pond. In Bangladesh, people fish. A lot. So, sometimes, I would fish at Grandma's pond. I remember when I was seven, I caught a big fish that almost broke the fishing rod I had. But I somehow still caught it. It was a pretty huge fish, and I felt really proud of that, like, "Hey, I'm the man!" It was pretty cool.

I was still in Rajshahi when I was nine years old. I went to an all-boys school. It was actually funny because, in Bangladesh, once you get to first grade, you have to take this test. It's an admissions test to see which high

31

school you will go to. High school goes from first grade to tenth grade in Bangladesh, and I actually ended up going to one of the top high schools in Rajshahi. I made some pretty good friends there. Because it was all boys, you can imagine how loud and rowdy it was every period. I made a lot of good friends at my high school.

I had it pretty good, even financially. It wasn't that much of a big deal, even though I didn't know how big the internet was before I got to the US. I didn't even have a computer, and our TV was one of those dinosaur TVs from back in the day, like when the first TVs came out.

My dad was pretty rich. But the bad thing was that my dad was super abusive to us. I can't remember one good memory that I had with my dad because he neglected me, my little brother, and my mom the whole time we were there. I remember some instances where he hit her. I remember being super angry, and I couldn't do anything because I lived there and I was little. So, I was like, "What can I do? I can't do anything." He never knew anything that was going on in my life. My mom would try to put up with it because she was more worried about mine and my brother's futures.

She put up with all that, and I don't know why. It was bad. It was terrible. My mom tried to make it better. But I guess it didn't work out.

It's been nine years since I left. I haven't talked to my dad. I haven't talked to him at all. I saw him once, later on. I went back to Bangladesh last summer. I saw him. It was . . . weird. I can't talk to him. We tried to talk, and I said, "I'm still mad about this stuff!" But, I've made my peace with that, and I'm okay now.

I don't like talking about it, but he did hit us. It's one thing when your parents discipline you. It's another thing when they hit you to release their own anger.

My mom is my role model for everything. Some people get the spotlight for what they do, but that wasn't important to her. She did it for us. I don't have a male role model in my life. Where I'm at right now is because of my mom. She took care of me. She looked after my education. She did it all by herself. And I look up to my mom so much. I put her up on a pedestal. One of my goals in life is to make sure my mom is happy, especially later on when she's old. Overall, life was pretty good, except for those parts.

How I got to the United States is actually a funny story. So, they had a Green Card lottery in Bangladesh. My uncle, my mom's younger brother, put our names in as a joke. He was like, "Ah, it's never going to hit us." We got the news two days later. We got picked! We won the lottery called DV. We had to go through all these processes. We were all like, "We can go to America!"

My mom still wanted to bring my dad. At that point, I said, "Why are you bringing him? We have to think of our future. He doesn't matter. We can take care of ourselves. We don't need his money. We'll get the money some-how." So, after we found out that we were going to America, my uncle took off a year from law school so he could help us with all the paperwork. And, there was a lot of paperwork.

Dhaka, the capital of Bangladesh, is where the embassy is. It's a five-hour journey from Rajshahi. It's because of how bad the roads are. Almost every other month, we'd go to Dhaka and stay at my aunt's house. Then we'd go to the embassy, do our paperwork, and go back. The doctors would do all these tests on us too. It was a lot of paperwork, hard work, and hassle.

When we got rejected the first time, it was because of my dad. We told him that for ID photos, he had to have a new one made. We had to give them pictures that are not any older than one month. So, we all had to take new pictures for our passports. We told our dad to give them a new picture, one that is no older than a month, but he didn't listen. He said, "Nah, this one I already have will be good." So, we turned in the papers, and we got rejected. I don't know why, but, I was little and, I don't know, I cried when this hap-pened. I was like, "What the—?" It was so frustrating!

I thought I would never go to America. So, I was super sad. My mom was sad too. She really wanted to give us a good future. It wasn't going to hap-pen if we stayed in Bangladesh because of all the corruption in the country. Everything was terrible.

If you ask my family, they will tell you that ever since I was little, I wanted to travel. I always wanted to explore outside of Bangladesh and see the world. I wanted to go to America. I wanted to go to France and to all of the UK. I read a lot of books about all these places. They all sounded cool.

My aunt is a lawyer. She found an immigration lawyer that wanted to help us. We paid the immigration lawyer close to a thousand . . . wait, not a thousand dollars. Actually, less than that. I don't know the exact conversion from the Bangladeshi taka. We paid them a certain amount, and they got us different paperwork. We filled it out. We reapplied, and we were accepted the next day, including my dad. My mom asked my dad, "Do you want to come so you can live with us?" She was worried that she wasn't going to be able to take care of us there. She wanted my dad to come so that we would have a good future. But my dad didn't want to go. I was like, "Alright." I was a little happy that my dad wasn't coming, mostly because my mom could not escape his tyranny.

I didn't feel like we were really going until the day we stepped into the airport. I'd never been to an airport before that time. I used to think that airplanes were super huge. I was a little disappointed seeing one in person. I was like, "Oh, they're not as big as I thought." It was still very fun. I was like, "Hey I still get to fly on a plane."

At the airport, I saw all these people that didn't look like me. They were all from different ethnic backgrounds. They looked different, and they were speaking their own languages. I was like, "Wow!" I even tried to talk to some of them!

But, not until I stepped into that airport, did I think, "Wow, I'm actually going!" Our flight went from Bangladesh to Dubai, and then it went to London. Then it came to America. It took almost a whole day—a little more than twenty-seven hours. That's when it first hit me that I would actually be an American.

I was riding around, and thought, "What the—? There's no rickshaws or anything! Rickshaws are a big thing in Bangladesh. It's all cars on the roads here!"

And the roads here are good—big roads, clean roads—with space! You see roads in Bangladesh and barely anything can fit on them. They're broken. They're one lane, and you'll see five cars in that one lane. So, when I saw the roads here, I thought it was pretty impressive.

My uncle was already here in Atlanta. He was the only family member I had here. We were planning to move in with him and my aunt for a while after we arrived here. I guess they were our anchor. So, we moved in with them the first day.

We stayed with my uncle for about a month. I was in DeKalb, and I went to Montclair Elementary School. I moved a lot while in elementary. I didn't like moving because I would make friends then have to leave them. It wasn't hard to make friends, but it still bothered me because every time I moved to a new school, I had that anxiety that you have. I thought, "Oh, new people. What do I do? I can't say the wrong thing or that's it. It's over. That's it."

When we moved to America, I had another fear. Around that time, people feared Muslims, even though I wasn't the stereotypical Muslim. I guess you can't tell by looking at me that I'm a Muslim. But there was still that fear. My mom was scared for us. I told her, "It is okay. Don't worry about it. We'll be okay. We're not bad people." But we still had that fear.

After staying with my uncle for a month, we moved to Forest Park. And that house, I tell you, was disgusting! I don't know why we moved there. It was just certain circumstances, like my mom's job was closer to that house.

So, we had to move there. The house was disgusting. It was full of roaches and rats, and we had to put out a lot of insecticide and rat traps, but it didn't do any good. I would get insect bites almost every other night. It was disgusting. It was a horrible condition, and I had to live like that for a whole year.

At that time, my mom got divorced from my dad. It took about two months. He signed the papers, and they were officially divorced. My mom met another guy, and they got married soon after that while we were still in Forest Park. And, yeah, that was my new stepdad. I was like, "Oh, okay, that's cool, I guess. Now I have a stepdad, and we're going to have some financial support."

When my new stepdad moved in with us, my uncle left the disgusting house. I don't know what happened, some kind of family fight or something. My family just drifted further apart from my uncle at that point. He didn't really support us. He didn't give us any money or anything. That relationship wasn't really there in the first place. So it's not like we were missing anything.

When I was in fourth grade, we moved again. We couldn't afford the mortgage on the disgusting house in Forest Park, so we moved to an apartment. I remember my stepdad didn't move in with us. He just left. He didn't say anything. He just left. He was gone. I asked my mom where he was. She didn't know. He was just . . . gone.

After he left us, it was just my mom, me, and my brother, and that was it. And we didn't know how we were we going to pay rent. It was hard. For a whole year, all we had to eat was just rice and potatoes. Sometimes we skipped lunch or dinner and had one meal a day. It was like this for a whole year. We did that because we had to pay rent or the landlord was going to kick us out. We had one room. That was it. We lived like that. Just me and my brother and my mom. But, we made the most of a bad situation.

After all that, my mom met another guy. They're married now. This guy is a pretty good, good, good guy. I guess he's my new stepdad. Hopefully, he isn't . . . I don't know. All this has made me not trust people so much. When I was younger, it was terrible. Now, things are better. This relationship has been stable. I can't complain about my life currently. My life right now is pretty good. I'm in a good place, financially too.

We pulled it together after we left Bangladesh. I felt what it's like to be like near poverty, even though I probably don't know what it feels like to be as poor as one of the kids in a third-world country. But, I know what it's like to not have money and struggle. That has made me more humble.

Currently, I'm working at Publix. For those who don't know, it's a lo-cal grocery store in the southern US. Sometimes, I help out my new stepdad financially or help look after my little brother. My stepdad helps out with the bills and takes really good care of my mom. My mom has a good job at Publix too. She works in the deli. We get pretty good pay.

School is going well. I'm trying to be a civil engineer. Once I graduate high school, I'll try to get accepted into Stanford. I love Stanford. This is one of my goals to go to Stanford and take classes. Stanford is actually pretty cool. It's got some cool perks. They have out-of-this-world labs and research facilities.

As for hobbies, I like . . . no, I mean, I love playing soccer. I grew up with Hispanics, and they taught me a lot of their culture: the food, the music, the dancing. Soccer was a big part of their culture; the soccer culture became a way of life for me. Even when I was in Bangladesh, the soccer culture was beautiful! I love the game! When I play it, my mind is cleared. I get really focused. Life is overall good right now.

When I went back this last summer to Bangladesh, I saw how the conditions were there. I saw it from a new perspective, now that I'm in a better place. How the people are there, the state they're in—it's terrible! I really want to do something about it once I get older. How can I give back? If I become a civil engineer, maybe I can make better designs to better preserve the environment or build better roads in Bangladesh someday. I don't know. But I also really want to help out the small countries that don't get attention from the bigger countries. I want to help out their communities. I think the smaller countries deserve more attention. They have people there too! This is how my life has been.

I think the American Dream is to help the world. We can't deny that we, America, are the superpower of the world. But we should not take that for granted. We should be using our power to help others. We can't . . . we shouldn't keep that gap that we have with other countries. We should try to help them close that gap. We should try to help other countries become better with their GDP and with all the hunger that's going on. We've got to. These people are being exploited. There's people over in Bangladesh and other countries, hungry, but we are wasting food. There are so many issues, and I alone can't tackle them. We need more people to be committed to tackling them. But what I can do is, at least, raise some awareness about all this. I felt what it's like to struggle, so I can't even imagine how other people feel in even more impoverished countries. I really want to look after the little guys; I want to help them out. And I think the American dream is to help other people and create a better world community.

If I had never left Bangladesh, I think I'd still be in the dark about how the world is. When I went there last summer and talked to the people in Bangladesh, even though they have internet, they don't realize how much they're struggling to live each day. They're okay with it. But when I see them from a different point of view, I feel they shouldn't have to go through all their struggles. They have their family, and they have a close community, and they feel good about it. But it's still a struggle with food. They shouldn't have to be struggling with food. They shouldn't have to be struggling with money. All these problems that they shouldn't have to struggle with, and we could help.

I just want to help the world become a better place, but it's frustrating that I can't do it all myself. I need more help. We need everyone to commit to it. I think for those who come here, we should look to helping others instead of taking what we have for granted. I think I'd just be another statistic like all the other people if I had stayed back in Bangladesh. I don't think I would dream this big. I think coming to America, losing all the money that my dad provided—losing all that—and struggling to work our way back up made me more humble about all that I have now. It made me more determined to help people that don't have anything.

VIDEO LINKS

greencardvoices.org/speakers/hm-sakib

Kalaymyo,
Myanmar

Dim Cing

From: Kalaymyo, Myanmar
Current City: Atlanta, GA

"FOOD IN MYANMAR IS SO DIFFERENT. IN MYANMAR, IF YOU CAN EAT MEAT ONCE IN A MONTH, THAT MEANS YOU ARE SO RICH. IN AMERICA, I CAN EAT MEAT EVERY DAY."

I'm from Myanmar. I was born in Kalaymyo. I used to live with my mom and my two sisters in a bamboo house. One day, when I was either five or six, soldiers came to my house, and they said they needed my older sister to be a porter. They wanted to make her carry their heavy things for them. She could not go with them because she has asthma and was not feeling well, but the soldiers said, "If you don't follow us, you guys know what we're gonna do." She was scared, so she just followed them. Then, at night, she ran away from the soldiers.

My mom asked my sister if everything was okay. My sister said, "No, I just ran from the soldiers." My mom was so worried about my sister and told her that she had to leave the country. If the soldiers saw her again, they might have killed her. My sister asked where she was going to live. My mom told her that she had to go to Malaysia. My sister agreed, and then she left. My mom started crying on her bed. I was sad that my sister had to leave.

A year later, my mom passed away. At that time, my grandma took care of one of my older sisters and me. My other sister was still in Malaysia. I didn't go to school when my grandma was taking care of me. I remember planting a garden of vegetables with her, and I would help take care of them.

Three years later, we got a call from my sister in Malaysia. We told her that our mom had passed away, and she cried on the phone. My grandma could not work anymore to support me and my sister, so she sent us to live with my other sister in Malaysia. I wanted to stay in Myanmar to be with my grandma.

I went to Malaysia, and I lived there for four years. In Malaysia, when my older sister had enough money, I could go to school. When she didn't have enough money, I couldn't go to school, so I just stopped going. On the days that I didn't go to school, I was learning how to read and write Burmese at home. My older sister taught me. When I lived in Malaysia, I would clean the church every Saturday. I also helped my church leader. He played guitar, and I helped to pluck the strings.

It was hard to find jobs in Malaysia, so my sister wanted to move. If we went to Myanmar, she would be killed by the soldiers, so we couldn't go back. She decided to go to America, so I had to follow her. She told me that in America you can have a better life.

We got a call from the UN Refugee Agency (UNHCR), and they told us that we had to do an interview to see if we could go to America. My older sister was so happy. I was like, "What's an interview?" I didn't even know what it was. We had to tell them about our story and why we had to leave Myanmar. We got accepted.

On the plane to America, I was thirsty, and the flight attendant asked if she could help me. I told her that I needed water, and she gave it to me. Then my older sister asked for Milo, and the flight attendant said, "What's Milo?" She didn't know what Milo was. It's a chocolate drink that is popular in Malaysia but not in America.

We landed in Atlanta. When I first saw American people, I thought they were so tall. My cousin's family was waiting on us in the airport. They had been in America for nine years. We hugged, and then we went and ate dinner together. I was so happy to be with them.

At first, we lived in an apartment in Atlanta. The apartments were so different than in Myanmar and Malaysia. Malaysian apartments are very tall, fifteen-floor buildings. In America, my apartment was only one floor. After a while, my sister didn't want to live in an apartment anymore, so then we moved in with my uncle and his family. Me and my two sisters moved into a house with them. At first, I thought it was so small, but when I walked inside, it was big. We had air conditioning at this house. When I lived in Malaysia, we did not have air conditioning, and it is so hot in Malaysia.

On my first day of school in America, I was so nervous. I was scared to talk to other students. They would talk to me, but I would keep to myself and just nod my head. I eventually made some friends, like I had in Myanmar. They are so good, and I was so happy. In school, I learn English, science, math, and social studies. Science is my favorite subject.

My favorite hobby is singing, but I'm too shy to sing in front of a lot of people. My favorite songs are Burmese songs and English songs. I like to sing Akon songs. I also like songs by a Burmese singer, Sai Sai. I like singing one of his love songs.

In America, my life is better than before in Myanmar because of the way we eat. Food in Myanmar is so different. In Myanmar, if you can eat meat once in a month, that means you are so rich. In America, I can eat meat every day. Here I can learn and find a job that I want. I have more opportunities to do what I want to do. If I didn't come to America, other people would try to find me a job. If they didn't have a job for me, I just wouldn't have a job.

I want to be a doctor, and I want to help sick people. When I see sick people, I feel bad. I don't like blood, but I want to become a doctor anyway because I love learning about science. I don't think I could have been a doctor in Malaysia or Myanmar because I couldn't go to school, and I couldn't do what I want to do. That's why I'm glad to be here in the US.

VIDEO LINKS

greencardvoices.org/speakers/dim-cing

Mexico City,
Mexico

Illustration by Yehimi Cambrón

Daniel

From: Mexico City, Mexico
Current City: Atlanta, GA

"THE AMERICAN DREAM IS TRUE BECAUSE IF WE HADN'T COME HERE, I WOULDN'T HAVE HAD THE EDUCATION I HAVE RIGHT NOW. I WOULDN'T HAVE THE OPPORTUNITIES AND THE EXPERIENCES I'M LIVING RIGHT NOW. BUT IT'S DEFINITELY HARD."

Where I'm from, we all get along. Everybody knows each other. I liked my life in Mexico. I lived with my mom because my dad was here in America. We weren't poor, but we weren't wealthy either. My mom and I would stay up until three in the morning packaging toy cars and stuff to sell. We would sell food cooked by my mom on the street. I lived with just my mom, and my grandparent's house was one house away so I got to see them a lot. I remember playing with my cousins. We had a soccer field right down the street. We would go most of the time. It was pretty hard because the only communication I had with my dad was by phone. I didn't remember anything about him. He left when I was two and was gone for about two years.

Then my dad returned to Mexico. He probably lived with us for about a year. It was decided we would be coming here to the US. I was four, about to turn five, when we left. It was out of nowhere. It was shocking to me because it was out of nowhere. I never expected to come here, and I was really sad, having to leave everything, like my family, behind: my grandparents, my cousins.

When we came to Atlanta, the only things we had were the clothes we had on. We moved into an apartment with my aunt, and we lived there for about one year until we moved out. My first days here, I knew no English. We didn't know where to go. Neighbors told us not to leave. I got sick, and we had no option but to leave. I remember the first time we actually bought clothes was at a yard sale. That was like the only clothes we had.

I started school two months after. I was really scared the first day. I didn't know anyone there. I remember my mom left crying when she dropped me off at school. She went back home crying because she said she was scared because I literally didn't know anything. It was really hard because I couldn't

43

understand anything they were saying. I got in trouble a lot for that same reason because I couldn't understand. The kids made fun of me because they knew more English than I did. But I made it through. It took me a month to learn English. I remember I had a lot of friends in kindergarten. I really had a lot of friends that supported me. They tried to teach me English. And to this day, I am still really close friends with most of them.

Now I feel like we are doing pretty good. We had a lot of struggles when we got here too, like money problems. After my mom gave birth to my second brother, my dad and I would literally go walking from our home all the way to Grady Hospital to see her because we had no money for a taxi or anything. My dad didn't have a job at that point, so he had to go stand on the corner and ask for jobs. That time was hard too. But now we are doing better, and I have actually worked for four years in construction with my dad. It's really hard too. He's been doing it for more than twelve years, and I only go over the summer. I can see how hard it is. I mean, that is the way I've been earning my money, like I try to earn my money the good way—working.

My favorite subject is social studies, and I play soccer as a hobby. Soccer means so much to me; it is my happiness. If I'm feeling stressed, or bored, or anything, I go to play soccer. I live every day like it is my last. The most special moment for me is when I just sit back with my dad and watch a game. You can expect to hear us scream when our team scores a goal, or jump out of our seat every time our team is on the attack. I still love soccer even though it has caused me to have two broken arms, a dislocated knee, a torn ligament, and many pulled hamstrings. That's just what I like to do all day.

I hope to go to Georgia Tech or Kennesaw State after I graduate. I want to be a computer engineer or immigration lawyer. I want to visit Madrid and would like to go back to Mexico City to visit my family one day. I really want to help my family out, repay them for all the things they've done for me. I also want to give back to my country because I am proud to be where I am from. I really want to give back to it.

With all honesty, I would not change anything from my past. All of my struggles have taught me lessons and have shown me how to be a much better person. From the poverty in Mexico to the struggles here in the US, I learned something from all of it. The unbelievable memories that I have of my friends—making fun of each other, or as we like to call it, "flaming" ourselves. I know this quote may be overused but those people really became my family. We have all had so many years of friendship.

I appreciate my family more than anything. They have done so much for me. My dad works nonstop to feed us, and my mom works so hard to keep us fed and keep the house clean; she is always the last one to sit down at the table to eat because she cares about us all so much. My two brothers, even though we fight a lot, I love them both so much and want to set the best example possible for them.

For me, democracy is basically freedom for everybody. Everybody gets to express themselves. Express their ideas. Choose a leader. The government doesn't have all the power. Freedom is being able to achieve what you want, what you set for yourself. As long as you follow the basic rules of the government, you can do anything you want.

I feel like the American Dream is true, but to a certain extent because I feel like people back in my home place feel like life here is easy. But it's not. There are a lot of struggles to be where we are now. Life was not as easy as they made it seem. The people I knew made it seem like it would be easy to progress here. But the American Dream is true because if we hadn't come here, I wouldn't have had the education I have right now. I wouldn't have the opportunities and the experiences I'm living right now. But it's definitely hard. It's not as easy as people think.

I know I'm going to be someone in life because I like putting my mind into the things I will accomplish. I will not stop until I reach my goals. I have made a promise to myself that I will not let all of the sacrifices my parents made for me go to waste. I want to be able to say that I came up from nothing and also always remain humble.

VIDEO LINKS

greencardvoices.org/speakers/daniel

Manila,
Philippines

Sean Cordovez

From: Manila, Philippines
Current City: Atlanta, GA

"I FELT VERY DIFFERENT, AND PEOPLE BULLIED ME, ACTUALLY TELLING ME I WAS DIFFERENT. AT FIRST IT MADE ME HATE THAT I WASN'T BORN HERE, BUT LOOKING BACK AT IT, I NOW FEEL UNIQUE AND PROUD THAT I AM DIFFERENT."

The memory of my life in the Philippines is not clear since I was a little kid during that time. My family says I used to be a quiet little boy who did not really do much because I was an introvert. When I was born, I did not have my dad around because he was already in America trying to set his life up and bring us there. It was hard for me whenever my dad was gone. When my dad visited me and my mom, they told me I turned into a different baby every time he was with us. I would laugh and giggle and be very happy. Whenever the time came that he would leave again, I would go back into that emotional state where I was quiet and more introverted. He would usually leave a baseball cap behind for me, and I would cry over the baseball caps because I knew I had a dad, but the caps reminded me he was not there with me. Those old baseball caps are still hanging there. My grandfather wears them sometimes to remind himself of me.

My dad helped us start the long process to come to America. My mom went through a ten-hour process at the embassy answering questions, taking tests about American history and speaking English, filling out so much paperwork, and paying a lot of money. It takes so much time and a lot of work to get through all of those things.

Once we found out we were going to the United States, my uncle bought a giant pig to celebrate, which is a festive thing in the Philippines and an indicator of a party. They closed off part of the streets, and old family friends, neighbors, and relatives all came to give us well wishes and say their farewells. We ate and talked all night, and at the end of the party, everyone was crying. My mom was restless the entire night before we left.

When we reached the airport, it was hard for my mom because my grandparents could only follow us until we got to the terminal. Then they waved goodbye, and my mom started crying. That's when my mom said it was hard because she had to bring me to America by herself with no help, and she barely knew English. She said it was one of the happiest and saddest days of her life, but she was happy for me to see that I would have a better chance in America than most kids would in the Philippines.

Our trip started from Manila, and then we had to fly all the way to Atlanta, which is around a sixteen-hour flight. As soon as we landed, my mom was scared, and I was scared. At three and a half years old, she saw me shaking a bit, so she reassured me to not be afraid and to be strong because my dad was coming.

When we got off the plane and out of the gate, we headed straight to baggage claim, and that is when I saw my dad. I ran past everyone standing in line and hugged my dad. I felt happy, and I felt safe with my family now that we were all together again as a whole for the first time in so long.

During my first impressions, I was skeptical and scared because some things were very different here in the US compared to the Philippines. My dad and my grandfather picked us up from the airport. They told me to put my seatbelt on, which I was not used to because in the Philippines seatbelts were not regulated as often, so we did not wear them as much as people do here in the US. That was one of my initial times getting used to American culture—safety regulations and seatbelts.

On the ride to the house, my dad and grandfather asked me many questions, so many that time passed by until I got to the house. Once we got there, I was shocked because in the Philippines we shared beds, and they had one toilet for eight different people, but now we have separate rooms to live in. As a kid, I thought this was pretty cool, but I didn't want to take it for granted. I remembered when we got off the plane that my mom always told me, "Don't forget where you came from, and don't forget to be modest of how you got here." Ever since she told me that, I always remind myself how important my home and family are to me. No matter where I go, I try to hold on to home, and I never forget all the sacrifices my family made for me to come to the US.

It was five days before my first American birthday, and my mom was finding a job because she at least wanted a cake for me. My dad wanted everyone to meet me, so my aunts and uncles came over for one whole day, and we had a birthday party. My mom cried because she hadn't seen her in-laws in a long time. They felt like a second family to her, but I had never met them, so I was scared and hiding behind my dad's leg. I held my dad's hand, and he introduced me to them. It was emotional for everyone.

Overall, getting used to America was pretty hard. I felt like an outsider, and I didn't feel welcomed initially. It was a long, long road to actually fitting in. I got to learn English as a second language, but I lost part of my

Tagalog because there weren't other Filipinos in the area except for my family, and it is hard to remember it all if you don't use it often. If there were other Filipinos around us, they never stayed there for a long time. I would make a few friends, and then they would leave. I never got to speak in Tagalog, so I prioritized learning English by watching all these little cartoons like *Dora the Explorer*. I read books and did workbooks even before Pre-K. I dedicated most of my early life to studying because I wanted to make my family proud and make sure that all the sacrifices my mom had to go through wouldn't be in vain. I felt like I had to work hard for them because they had done so much for me.

It was hard for me to adjust and find friends as an introvert in elementary school because I tried to stay humble. In Pre-K, I literally stumbled over my first American friend, and his name was Willie. I tripped over him, and he thought I was picking on him, so he threw a punch and hit me in the right eye. After the teacher scolded him, we made up and became friends. It might sound strange that a punch made us become friends, but we were just kids who did not know any better. Me and him would hang out most days, and I felt happy. He left during the fourth grade, and I felt so sad and doubtful that I would find another friend like him. But looking back on all the memories, Pre-K on to fourth grade was a blast.

Luckily in fourth grade, we got the chance to head back home to the Philippines. My mom had been saving a lot of money to bring me, my little sister, herself, and my dad to the Philippines and visit everyone. For seven years, we had been getting used to things in America, seven whole years that I had not been to my home country. My mom would call everyone back home every night and tell them about my achievements. She also told them how hard it was for me to make friends, but I was scared to go back home. I was scared because I wondered what the people back home would think of me after living in the US for so long.

The trip was the same route as before, Atlanta to Manila, but with some layovers in South Korea. It was about a three-hour ride to get home from the airport, and we got home around one in the morning where everyone was waiting for us. The ones greeting me were, ironically, the people we saw last: my grandfather, my grandmother, and my aunt. They all ran up to us and hugged us. It felt rejuvenating, and I felt at home. During that entire month that passed by, I felt happy and relaxed and ready to go back to the US for fifth grade.

Middle school was one of my toughest and saddest times growing up. I felt very different, and people bullied me, actually telling me I was different. At first it made me hate that I wasn't born here, but looking back at it, I now feel unique and proud that I am different. I accept who I am, and I am very proud to be Filipino.

This led me to eighth grade when I came out of my shell, joined activities, and made friends. I found a group that made me feel like I belonged, and I found friends I could relate to that I still talk to in high school. Those people helped shape me into the person I am today. I went from being shy and introverted to being much more outgoing. I had many different experiences with these new friends. Sometimes we would laugh with each other. Other times we would cry with each other. I felt like I could vent to them when I needed to, and they felt like they could vent to me too. It can take a long time to fit in with people. When I think about the times I spent with my friends, I am just so thankful that they were in my life. All of their stories brought us closer together, and they continue to inspire me to this day.

High school has been a grind so far. Me and my friends have been doing our best in school, and we are all a little bit anxious about our future because we are essentially at the starting line. There is so much for us to go out and do with our lives. All the sacrifices that my family made has brought me to this point in my life. I'm happy that they taught me everything I know about family, hope, and having faith. They told me, "If you believe in yourself, you will get there." So I know I will be able to get to where I want to in life as long as I believe in myself.

I feel so proud that I can make my family smile because of my achievements, but I do not want to stop there. I really want to make them happier by making their life easier because I know it is much harder over there in the Philippines than it is here. Life there is way tougher, and they have much more of a struggle just in their daily lives. It has toughened them up, and now I am trying to toughen up as well. It is tough for so many people like me because we are trying to make a foundation for ourselves, trying to make a name, and trying to repay our debts to the people we love. So I'm happy that I get to be here in the US, and I will take advantage of the opportunities I have here.

Here in America I have more resources to play with compared to what I would have had in the Philippines, which has helped me want to become a biomedical engineer. As a kid I was very interested in tinkering with robots and stuff like that. Now I realize I also want to find a way to help people who are struggling. Wanting to help people has always been one of the biggest parts of my personality. I feel a warm sense of accomplishment when I connect with a person, make them smile, or help someone. That love of helping people drew me into community service groups like the National Honor Society for high school students and Beta Club. I feel very proud that I can give back to people. So the compromise I found was studying biomedical engineering. It is a growing field that is challenging yet fun. I feel like it will give me an opportunity to combine my love of helping people with my love of robotics and engineering.

I want to be able to send a cut of my paycheck back to my family in the Philippines until I can save up to go back and help my grandparents move out of the crowded city. Ultimately, my dream is to help them build the house they want in the suburbs and be able to have the rest of our family live together with them.

It has been a long road getting here and it's a longer road up ahead. I don't know what's up there, but so far it has been a ride. I'm happy that I get to be here in the US. I have said that so many times, but I really am. It makes me proud that I can make my family proud. One of my motivations that keeps me going is my family. I promise one day I will go back with something to repay them all for all their sacrifices. Coming back home and making their lives easier for the ones that are still back home—that is my promise to them.

VIDEO LINKS

greencardvoices.org/speakers/sean-cordovez

Dhaka,
Bangladesh

Dania Karim

From: Dhaka, Bangladesh
Current City: Atlanta, GA

"YOU NEVER KNOW HOW MUCH YOU MISS SOMEONE UNTIL THEY'RE NOT WITH YOU ANYMORE."

My childhood was really fun because I had a lot of cousins to play around with and we have a giant family. My favorite thing about Bangladesh was my family. On occasion, we would have picnics. We would all come over and eat together. We would celebrate birthdays, weddings, and holidays. It was grand. Our houses were right next to each other, separated by families. My uncle lived in one house and then my dad. The other uncles and aunties would be living nearby too. It was really easy to meet each other. It was not the most popular neighborhood—the situation was neutral, but when I was little, I heard about fights and stuff.

My family started preparing really early to move to America. We didn't sell any properties because my grandpa didn't distribute the property properly when he passed away so we didn't own any properties back then. I went to a special school. It's for English learning. It was for a year. I was in regular school, but then I moved to the special school to learn more English. At that school, I was able to catch up with other students. That's how I learned English so fluently, I guess. I didn't have much trouble when I came to America because I already knew a bit of English.

One day, I was at school, and when I came back, Dad was like, "We got the call that we are getting the visa, and then we'll have to go to the certain place to receive it." At first, I thought it was not going to happen because we had been waiting for so long. We applied when I was like two years old. I was really young. After that, we went through a real process. We went to the embassy many times. We had to drive to a different state. We would rent a car and stay with my uncle for the night. The trips were long and tiring. So, when I heard the big news, I was so surprised. Like, "Whoa, we're going to America." It's a big deal because our other cousins were there already so it will be nice to meet them again.

We had a party, and my relatives came to say goodbye. I didn't know what was going on, so I was happy. I was cheerful. I was like, "Yay! We're finally leaving. It has been our big dream to move to America and it's really happening." I wasn't sad at that time. When I arrived at the airport, I started crying because it was like, "I'm seriously leaving and I can't go back now." It was really upsetting. I was crying the whole way, but when I arrived, I was like, "Okay, calm down." It's just . . . we have to face it.

We packed everything up and mailed it to my uncle. On the plane, we took only our clothes. First, we came to New York because our aunt lived there, and there was something wrong with our flight. It got canceled, so we had to get another plane ticket to Atlanta because that was our final destination. We stayed there for one night, and then in the morning when everything was ready, we came to Atlanta.

My dad's distant relative was waiting for us. He lives here with his family, and he recommended Atlanta. We wanted to go to Michigan, but it's too cold there. So we were like, "Let's just go to Atlanta instead," and he was really supportive. We chose Atlanta because we were convinced that it was the best place for us to start with.

When we landed and made it to the apartment, we all went out. It was surprising. We were like, "Oh, what's going on?" There were like lots of people around. There were Hispanic, Black, White—all kinds of mixed people. This was the first time I had seen all those people, and I was moved. I was like, "Whoa, they look so different from me."

After that, I went to Sequoyah Middle School. When I went to school, it was a whole different experience because they weren't like me. They had their own style of hair, clothes, and everything. I was like, "Wow, this is something brand new." I felt like I discovered a whole new world. The adjustment was difficult. Coming to America, I had a phobia. It was first really hard to make friends because I was shy. I wasn't approaching everyone and talking to everyone. Then, I met some friends. Some of them were from my country, so it was easy to get along with them.

I am in high school now, and my favorite extracurricular activity is listening to music. I'm not in any school clubs because I'm too shy, and there are too many people. I still have a phobia around people. I get nervous. It's really hard to handle it, so I chose not to join any school clubs because of that. I'm also not very athletic, so I avoid sports. The education system in America is better. In Bangladesh, school was getting hard. I knew that if I stayed, I might not have the brightest future. I've thought about being a teacher. I'm not sure of the career I want. I feel like that's not going to be an issue because America is a place with many better opportunities.

I never really thought much about the American Dream before. But now that I think about it, it feels like something that has a greater purpose in our lives; something that could change us into someone important; someone who contributes to the society. If I stayed in Bangladesh, I wouldn't be working at this age. In our country, you are not allowed to work until you graduate college unless you open your own business, but that's rare for females to open a business of their own. Mostly males take the lead. They are the big shots. I wouldn't be working at this age, so that's the real difference. My grades would not be the way they are now. Now, my parents have expectations and they want me to be someone in the society. They want me to have a career of my own. And I'll not disappoint them.

While being in America, I discovered many things that I didn't know. I barely knew that Mexico is a country that existed. I barely knew any countries that existed. When I was in my country, my world was very tiny. It was like, "There's China, there's America, there's Britain, and that's it." I didn't think much because I was a kid. After coming to America, I discovered so many things that I'm passionate about. I found out about anime. I watch it all the time. I love American television shows like fantasy: the characters, the background music, the sceneries. It's all so beautiful. I also found out that I love Korean music.

The hardest part about moving to America is missing my family. I text them and sometimes I just don't know what to say. You never know how much you miss someone until they're not here with you anymore. The best part about moving was that I learned so much I didn't know before. My personality and everything has changed. I know I wouldn't be the person I am today if I didn't move here. Most of the time, I don't think about the future. The present is more suitable. We'll see what happens next—for better or for worse.

VIDEO LINKS

greencardvoices.org/speakers/dania-karim

Illustration by Yehimi Cambrón

Tijuana,
Mexico

Luis

From: Tijuana, Mexico
Current City: Atlanta, GA

> "ALL THESE OBSTACLES ARE THERE FOR A REASON. OBSTACLES ARE MADE TO BE OVERCOME. YOU HAVE TO PERSEVERE."

I was born in Tijuana, Baja California in Mexico. That's literally the border-line between the US and Mexico. I could've been born in the US any second.

My life, as I remember in Mexico, is very vague. There is not a lot I can say about it because I came to the US when I was five years old. I remember when I was two that I went to the beach where my grandma used to live. I remember every day we would go to the beach and enjoy it with our family. I love the water. They would tell me that I would go into the water, and I would never get out. My dad left us when I was three years old, and ever since, he has never been in my life. So, my mom has played a huge role in my life, playing both the father and the mother role.

When I was seven months, my mom moved to US and stayed with her friend in San Diego, California for a while. She worked double shifts every day for seven straight months, trying to get the money for me to come. She told me that every day she would cry at night because she missed her family so much, and she was very scared. She had a lot of obstacles because she didn't know any English. It was also very difficult for her since she didn't know the city or have any family there, and she didn't have me with her.

When I came here to the US, I came here by airplane. I don't remember a lot because I was five years old. I remember just getting off the plane. Sadly, my mom wasn't the one that picked me and my cousin up. It was my mom's friend that she was living with because my mom had to work a double shift. That day, when I finally saw my mom, I was so happy I started crying. I ran up to her and gave her a hug. She started crying. I remember she told me that she didn't sleep at all. I still remember that even though I'm eighteen now. The first day that we saw each other again, we just clicked, and ever since that day, I have not been away from my mom. That same night, my cousin

57

and I were amazed at how different the country is. I was with my cousin who was three, and I was just five years old. We were just little kids, and we were just crazy like, "Oh my gosh! Where are we? It's just so cool!"

We were in California for two months; then we moved to Tennessee. I'm never going to forget Knoxville, Tennessee in particular. I started kindergarten there. I remember my first words I learned were "cat" and "dog." I remember everywhere I would go, if there was a cat or dog, I would say, "Eso es un gato," meaning "that is a cat." I would be like, "Eso es un cat! Eso es un dog." I lived in Tennessee until fourth grade. I really didn't know how different my circumstances were from other kids. I didn't know I was undocumented.

I was going to fifth grade when my mom told me we will be moving to San Francisco, California. For me, it was amazing. I saw the Golden Gate Bridge and many other attractions. I started at my new school in California. I was at the top of the food chain as a fifth grader. I had classmates from Pakistan, Algeria, Venezuela. I didn't feel very isolated because my school was diverse and accepting. I enjoy meeting new people and learning about their cultures. I lived two blocks away from my school. We were in the city where everyone would pass by, and there was a lot of tourism going on. I remember that every morning I would always get annoyed because when I would go to school, I would have to walk by myself with other students that lived around me and tourists would always ask, "Where do we go? Direct me." And I'm over here like, "I don't even know where I'm going. I can't help you." Rent and everything was expensive in San Francisco. I used to live on top of a laundromat. I would have to go through the laundromat every day just to get to my apartment. Every day and night, we would feel rumbling.

In my school in San Francisco, I was part of our soccer team. Our team was really good, and we were going to the finals of the tournament. I remember that on the night before the finals, we had soccer practice. My mom took forever to come pick me up. The coach was ready to go home. She was calling my mom, but my mom was not picking up. Then suddenly, my mom popped up, and she told me that we had to move again. I felt heartbroken that I had to leave behind friends that I was becoming close to.

Next thing you know, we were on a airplane on our way back to Tennessee. I left everything there. To this day, I actually feel bad that I could not say bye to my friends. I was nine years old, and I was so confused. After that, we were living in rural parts of Tennessee. My mom was still having a lot of problems with racism and finding a good job. We weren't living in the city compared to San Francisco. I was the new student again. That was my name. I got used to that. After one month, we went to Richmond, Kentucky because my mom's sister lived there. My aunt had a good job over there. We still moved a few times. I went to three different elementary schools in fifth grade because of that. I got used to always seeing new faces and not knowing where to go. I was lost. I was in Kentucky for five months. I was really confused because I was moving so much that I couldn't even have a normal life. Like I said, my new name was "New Student."

After Kentucky, we moved to Atlanta. I was a new student again. I started going to school at Garden Hills in fifth grade. So in total, I went to seven different elementary schools just in fifth grade. Even though I went to so many different schools, I still learned a lot because of my drive to work hard and continue working hard. Everyone was so shocked with how much I knew for someone that was a new student constantly. My mom loved it here in Georgia, and to this day, we are still here. I can say that coming to Georgia has been a big impact in my life. Atlanta, Georgia was a big help in developing who I am now.

I didn't work until I was in eleventh grade because my mother didn't need the help. She was independent. All she wanted me to do was work hard in school and be a leader. When I was a freshman, at thirteen years old, I had to start helping out my mom more often because she was getting a little older. She had been working since she was fourteen years old. So she'd been working non-stop until this time when she was forty years old.

After eighth grade graduation, everything was looking up. I was excited to be a freshman in high school. I thought, "Four more years and I'm done." I can actually start becoming who I want to be in life. Freshman year was cool. I was doing good in my classes. I was enjoying high school.

One day when I was thirteen years old, me and my mom were coming home from the store. We were next to a street on the sidewalk, and a car stopped to let us pass by an intersection. Another car hit the first car from behind, which then hit into us. I was pulling my mom slowly because I could see the car while we were talking. By the time I noticed it, the car was about to hit us. I pulled my mom really hard, but next thing you know, she got hit by a car in front of my very own eyes. The force of the car hitting my mom flew her out of my hand. I saw my mom fly in the air like a ball. She bounced twice. I didn't know what to do because I had so many emotions running through my head.

I finally reacted after seeing my mom on the ground. I ran towards her. I was shaking her while shouting, "Mama, Mama." I was panicking. The car, which hit the car in front that hit us, fled the scene. The guy that hit us, but only because the guy who fled had hit him, walked out of the car. I didn't know at that moment that he wasn't the one to blame for what happened. He came at me and asked if I was okay. I thought it was his fault, and I was mad to the point where I wanted to hit him. He started walking toward my mom. Thinking that he did this, I started pushing him away, blocking my mom with my own body. That is when he tried to explain to me that it wasn't his fault. My mom was still on the ground unconscious. The other people who saw what happened were trying to help and people started calling 911. I was still angry, sad, and scared. I didn't know what to do, and I was traumatized completely.

The ambulance came, and they picked her up. One of the ambulance workers told me that when they were picking up my mom, I was on top of them. I was like, "Hey, please don't grab right there!" I was telling professionals how to grab my mom because I was scared they were going to hurt her more than she already was. Her ear was scraped badly, and she hit her head very hard. Luckily, she did not have any brain damage even though it was a really drastic crash. When they put her in the ambulance, I wanted to go with her. They told me I couldn't. I remember screaming at them, trying to get them to let me come. Luckily, the driver could see how much I really wanted to be with her and took me with her.

When we got to the hospital, I couldn't go back with her. I had to wait in the waiting room for the longest forty minutes of my life. I was still traumatized, but I had to think fast about what I was going to do. I had her phone with only two percent battery left. I took down some important numbers before it died so that I could contact people from another phone.

When I could go see her, I ran. They said walk, but I ran anyway. I ran as fast as I could, running until they got more mad. I had to see where she was and know what was wrong with her. When I saw her, I started crying. I wanted to go hug her, but the nurse said I couldn't. She didn't break any bones, but she did get hit in the back. Her spine hit her heart. That's why she was in very critical condition.

Suddenly, my mom turned around on the bed and looked at me. She smiled, even though half her face was bleeding, and said, "It's going to be okay." In that moment, I was shocked to hear that. Then she looked at me again and she told me, "Trust me, it's gonna be okay." After she told me that, she went unconscious again. That's the last thing she wanted to tell me before she knocked out for the whole night. At that moment, I was so shocked, as she was telling me these things in this condition. Even when she knew she was in pain and almost dying, she was still trying to keep me calm. Even when I was physically okay, but mentally I was dying. I didn't know what to do. I was confused. I wanted to hug her again, but I couldn't do it.

After that, I wanted to stay the night with her. I was sleepy; I was tired. I was scared. I was everything. My phone had no battery. Everything was going bad in this moment. I hoped and hoped that everything went well with her. I hoped she wouldn't die.

Then, my uncle came to pick me up around midnight. He said I had to leave because I had school in the morning. He stayed there for an hour and a half telling me to leave, and I was telling him, "I'm not leaving." But the doctor told me I had to go home. It was not healthy to stay with my mom. My uncle said that he did feel a little happy for me, knowing that in these tough times I didn't just want to leave my mom there. I wanted to stay there like a loyal son with my mom. In the end, I went home with him. Knowing that the one person that was in my life, my only family member, was almost about to die, that may be the worst. I thought to myself, "What am I gonna do? I'm barely thirteen. I don't even know how to do my own laundry. How am I gonna survive if my mom dies? I'm done, I'm done, that's it."

When I got home with my uncle, I was knocked out. I saw a bed; I went to sleep. He said it was the fastest he's ever seen me go to sleep in his life. I was dying mentally. The next morning I went to school, but I didn't want to be there. My mind was somewhere else other than school, even in my favorite classes. I was planning my future if my mom didn't make it. After school, I went to see my mom, and they told me that she was okay. She was responding to all the exams they were doing, but she had to stay in the hospital for two months. She was still in critical condition, and I couldn't stay with her because there was no one to take care of me in the hospital. So I had to go home by myself. My mom gave me the keys and four-hundred dollars. She gave me her debit card and everything I needed. From that moment, I was literally independent for two months.

For those two months, it was crazy. I had to do everything by myself. In those two months, I learned what an adult learns in three years because I had to. If I didn't do these things, I wasn't going to survive. So, I learned how to cook, and I learned how to wash my own clothes. The first day I went to wash my own clothes, I put too much soap in, and I had a big bath of soap coming out of the washer, but I learned how to do it. I learned how to clean up by myself. I learned how to clean the bathroom. I did cry a lot. I was still sad. I was still scared. The only thing that kept me going was my mother— that was it—my mother. When all these things were going on, I would re-member that she said, "It's going to be alright." Every time I was falling down, I remembered what she said, and I kept going.

I would go visit my mom whenever I could. I would go on the bus late at night. I would wake up late for school because I would go visit my mom and get home at like 5:00 in the morning. Most of the money that my mom gave me, I used to go visit her.

When two months passed by, she was able to come back home with me. I was happy. It was like when I first saw her when I came from Mexico. I got the same feelings because we got to be together finally. Ironically, we went to a theme park when she came out. She didn't go on any of the rides, but we went together. We enjoyed ourselves. She told me, "I'm proud of you, son. I'm proud of everything you overcame." She asked me, "What motivated you to keep going?" And I told her, "It's you, Mom. You gave me everything I needed to survive. Every lesson you told me, every time you got mad at me for doing something wrong. All those things helped me out to make me how I am." My mom getting hit by a car was tough, but it taught me many important lessons.

Now I am a senior in Cross Keys High School. I am a boxing trainer and front desk receptionist. I have been working there for a year now. I train kids as little as seven year olds to people that could be my own parents. I sell memberships and all the tools you need. I tell people about the gym. So I'm literally the face of the gym. I also do the social media pages for the gym. I work every day after school. Even though I get out at 9:30 at night, I still find ways to do homework, study, have time for myself, have time for my mom. That's what I do most of the time. I'm also part of school clubs including National Honor Society for high school students, and I spend time doing community service. I train as a boxer and wrestler, and I practice Muay Thai. All of these things keep me motivated. I am also in the top ten percent of my grade, and to me that's amazing because it shows everything that I've done to this point is paying off now.

In the future, I might want to become a physical therapist. When my mom got hit by a car, I had to give her a lot of massages, and I noticed I am actually pretty good at them. I enjoy giving people massages because I like to make people feel better. But there are plenty of other things I will do. I feel I have the potential to do many extraordinary things in the community. I want to do more dancing because I love to dance. I will become more of a leader. I will become a role model for people. I will be able to show people that it doesn't matter where you are from; it doesn't matter what race you are. It only matters how hard you want it and how hard you work for it. All these obstacles are there for a reason. Obstacles are made to be overcome. You have to persevere.

In general, I want to find positive things in people's lives, and I want to emphasize them because some people might go through what I'm going through, or something even worse. I want them to feel like they can overcome it without having to feel like that is the end, like that is where their life ends.

VIDEO LINKS

greencardvoices.org/speakers/luis

Kabul,
Afghanistan

Farhat Sadat

From: Kabul, Afghanistan
Current City: Atlanta, GA

"COMING HERE TO AMERICA SAVED MY FAMILY AND ME. I DON'T HAVE TO LIVE IN A BAD SITUATION ANYMORE. MY LIFE IS VERY GOOD HERE."

My name is Farhat. I'm from Afghanistan. I'm seventeen years old. I speak Persian. I have six siblings—two brothers and four sisters. In October of 2016, I came to America. When we first heard that we would be coming to America, we were all very happy and excited. Our family moved here because our country is not good.

My father was working in America for the past ten years. At first, my father worked three jobs in the United States—one of them at a carpet company—but he hurt his hand. It became a problem because he was in so much pain, so he took a new job at a farmers' market. He loves that. He enjoys it. He's happy.

For me, it was very hard to leave because I had to say goodbye to all of my family in Afghanistan. I left my uncle, aunt, and all my other family there. I saw each of them one last time before I came to America. We left Afghanistan on a plane to come to America. The plane ride to the United States was good. We landed in Atlanta.

When I first came to America, I didn't know what the situation would be like here. I had always thought that the American people would be kind and that they would help each other. I always thought the people in America were very beautiful. After getting here, I saw that I was right. But when I came to America, it was so confusing. Everything was new for me.

My case manager is a very good woman, and she is very helpful to my family. When we first arrived, she worked a lot with my family to make us comfortable here. I didn't understand how to do things here in America, but she helped me. She is a very good woman. I like her, and I'm very happy in America.

When I came here, I talked with the American people, and they were kind. I knew that my family would be safe here. But when I came to America, I could not speak English. For me, it was very hard, but I can see that the American people were trying to help me. I could tell it was a very happy place. My family was safe.

I'm very happy I came to America because the situation in Afghanistan is very bad. The Taliban is fighting with my people and that makes it not safe. A lot of my people have died. In Afghanistan, I didn't have a good school. I didn't have a good hospital. I couldn't have a job. My family had economic problems. The people there were not safe. It was very bad. There were so many problems in Afghanistan.

Afghanistan is very different from America in a lot of bad ways. I didn't have any opportunities there. In Afghanistan, being a woman is not good. It's difficult for women to go to school. In Afghanistan, school is different from school in America. Boys and girls go to different schools, and the schools in Afghanistan don't have any computers or books. In Afghanistan, the teaching isn't as good. Hospitals in Afghanistan are not good because they don't have good technology or electronic devices, so doctors have problems helping people. When people are fighting and dying, there's not enough room for all of them. The hospitals are not big.

Coming here to America saved my family and me. I don't have to live in a bad situation anymore. My life is very good here. Now I have a good school. I have a good hospital. It's all very good. I am very happy that I came to America.

Here in America, I go to a good school, but I could not speak in English when I first arrived. So when I came to school, I was very scared. I was nervous. I didn't understand English, so I went home and cried. I said, "I don't like this school. I'm not going to this school. I don't understand English." But one day, I was going to school, and I saw people. I talked to those people. My first friends were two girls. I met them a week after I came to America. They were both from other countries too. They talked to me. When I had a problem, they helped me. But I miss them because they're at another school now.

My teacher was a very kind lady and helped me. I liked her. I am happy at school now. I'm happy that my teachers always help me. I'm very happy that I came to America. My favorite subject is math, but my favorite teacher taught geography. I liked learning about landforms, landscapes, cultures, and religions in her class. I liked to listen to her talk because when she spoke, I understood everything. She was a good teacher. But all the teachers I have had here are so good.

I also like the food at the cafeteria here at school. American food is good, but I think food in Afghanistan is better. Food from Afghanistan is so delicious and good. Kabuli Palaw rice is my favorite food from Afghanistan, and pizza is my favorite food in America. I like to eat pizza with vegetable toppings. It's very good.

When I'm not in school, I study English all the time. I study so many words. I'm scared because I cannot speak English very well, so I study it at home. I get so tired, but I watch videos in English to learn more. My goal is to graduate as a good student with good grades, and I want to speak very well. I just hope I'll keep being a student. I want to go to college one day and be an accountant.

In Afghanistan, I knew I wanted to be an accountant, and I want to be an accountant here in America too. I want to be an accountant because I like math. Math is easy for me. One day, I hope I'll be very good at accounting. I want to be an accountant to help all the people in my American community and the community back in my country. I like to help people.

VIDEO LINKS

greencardvoices.org/speakers/farhat-sadat

Istanbul,
Turkey

Edanur Isik

From: Istanbul, Turkey
Current City: Atlanta, GA

"WHEN I GOT TO THE ATLANTA AIRPORT, I FELT LOST. I HAD LEFT EVERYTHING BEHIND. I WOULD GO TO SCHOOL WITH NO FRIENDS. I DID NOT KNOW THE LANGUAGE. I DID NOT KNOW THE PEOPLE. I DID NOT KNOW THE CULTURE."

I was born in Istanbul. Istanbul is a big city—it's noisy, crowded, and traffic is really bad and not as quiet as here in Atlanta. Still, I think it is the most beautiful city in the world. I lived all my life there in an apartment with my family. The apartment was close to my grandparent's house. As a child I enjoyed spending time with them during the weekends. They were so old that they didn't spend a lot of time outside of their house. Because of that we found fun stuff to do at home, such as playing cards and watching soccer and talk shows on TV.

Since my birthday is on New Year's Day, we would celebrate my birthday and the new year at the same time. I enjoyed those nights so much. As I grew older, those family parties started getting smaller, and instead I had spent those nights with my friends. On one of my birthdays, we played this game called Tombala. It's like bingo. It is a game we only played on New Year's and you need five or more people for the game. We were dancing and watching fireworks and just having a lot of fun. They were good friends.

I went to the schools in our neighborhood, so I didn't have to spend a lot of time in traffic. I was always a good student and got good grades in elementary and junior high. My teachers liked me. My parents were proud, and I had many friends. Right before I came to America, I was a senior in junior high, and I had to study so hard to get a good score on the high school entrance exam. The test was very hard. There were 240 questions. If you made more than two mistakes, you could not go to a good school. There are special classes you can take or you can study by yourself. Family helped too. To prepare, I was not only going to school but also taking some private lessons where we had lots of practice about this big test. Because of my preparations, my score was not too bad, and I was able to enter a decent school.

We had two types of school in Turkey: government school, or public school as it is called in America, and private school. If you wanted to go to a good government school, you had to get a perfect score on the test you took right before you graduated junior high. If you wanted to go to private school, you should have made a good score and had a lot of money. They are very expensive. It was not possible for my family to send me to private school even though I had gotten a good score, so I had to leave Turkey to get a better education in the States.

One of the best days of my life was when we had the junior high graduation party. It was my very first night out with my friends and was so special because my parents usually did not allow me to be outside after 7:00 pm. The party was unbelievable. We had food, drinks, and we danced all night. We took lots of videos and photos. We sang songs. It was a night I will never forget. It was the first party I had in Turkey and also the last party I had. For me it was special because it was going to be the last time I would have so much fun with my friends before leaving for America.

I was nervous and sad to leave. I was sad because I would not see my friends and family for a long time. It would be my first time being away from them, and I didn't even know when I would see them next. I was nervous because I would not be able to communicate with people since I didn't know English. I knew that making friends at first would be impossible. I was a little happy though because I was going to live with my half-sister, who had moved away from home by the time I was born.

I went to the Istanbul airport with my family. I was crying, and my mom saw me crying so she started crying too. We were going to miss each other a lot, but we knew I had to go. So we said goodbye, and I got on the airplane with my older brother, who was coming for his vacation to visit our sister, and we went to America together. He stayed in America for one month before going back to Turkey. When I got to the Atlanta airport, I felt lost. I had left everything behind. I would go to school with no friends. I did not know the language. I did not know the people. I did not know the culture. Imagine if you were at a place you have never seen before and you were alone, if you were a stranger and if everything is strange. That is how I felt.

I was very sad and thinking about my mother and my father and my friends too. I miss them a lot, but I talk to my parents every day. There is an eight-hour time difference. I met my brother-in-law at the airport, and he took me and my brother to our sister's house. It was dark outside and very quiet. When I saw my sister and my little nephew, I was very happy. I felt that I was not going to be totally alone. I was also very tired from the fourteen-hour flight. The flight went from Turkey straight to Atlanta. The first thing I did was go to sleep.

The next day I went to the hospital with my sister to get shots so I wouldn't get sick. I don't like shots, but I knew I had to get these shots or I couldn't go to school. I had to get six shots and they hurt a little, but I knew it was so I could be safe. After that, I went back home. I wanted to know my family here better, so I started playing with my little nephew. He was four or five months old then. Now he is eleven months old. After I played with him, I would call my friends in Turkey. I cried to my best friend, but I tried to stay tough when talking to my other friends. We talked about how life was so different here, about how I miss them, and about how they miss me. It was very heartwarming, and I felt a little better after talking to them. I still talk with them a lot even now.

I started to go to school two days after I came to America. I was so anxious and a little bit scared because I could not speak English. I was scared because maybe they would laugh at me and not like me, but I shouldn't have been so scared. I started school at the DeKalb International Student Center, and I made friends on my first day, and things were good. I met them in the classroom, and we got to talk more when we went to lunch. At lunch, they tried to teach me a little English, and I guessed they liked me, so we became friends. We talked in what little English we knew. They were international students too. They were from Afghanistan and Ethiopia and they helped me a lot on the first day. My voice at first was so quiet. I was afraid and shy of letting people hear my voice, but they kept trying to talk to me. I got more confident. Now that I know a lot more English, I try not to hide my voice as much. I talk as much as I can and I answer a lot of questions in class.

I was at the International Center for five months and then I took a test. After I took the test, I got transferred to Cross Keys High School. I like it better here at Cross Keys. I am able to learn English more and talk with native speakers. I am currently in the ninth grade.

Everything in America is different: food, schools, people, city life. Everything was totally different from Turkey. To help adjust to America, I started to learn English. Making friends and being able to communicate with people helped me a lot. At first, I thought I would never be able to order food at a restaurant by myself or ask somebody for help if I got lost. As time passed, I started understanding people, and this made my days a lot easier. I learned a lot of English from watching television, talking to friends from school, reading some books, and listening to music.

I also started swimming and watching local soccer games. Soccer is a big thing back home, just like football in this country. I am a big fan of the neighborhood soccer team, and me and my family go to their games often since the stadium is a fifteen-minute walk from my house. I also want to start playing tennis with my friends, and I hope that we can become better friends that way.

I like to visit different places and meet new people. I go with my friends a lot to the mall to do shopping, and I like to look at makeup stuff. Sometimes, I put makeup on and take a picture of myself to send to friends, and we talk about how pretty we look. I read a lot about different makeups, healthier stuff to use, different tricks, and so on. I can't wait until I'm old enough to try makeup on in public. My hobbies are shopping and listening and singing along to music. My favorite singers are Turkish singers. They're Sezen Aksu and Sila.

Now I feel okay about living here. Not only can I speak English better, but I also know a lot of people. I have friends now whom I will miss if I ever go back to Turkey, but I also have friends that I miss so much in Turkey. In other words, life here is not as hard as it used to be.

VIDEO LINKS

greencardvoices.org/speakers/edanur-isik

Pokhara,
Nepal

Sanjith Yadav

From: Pokhara, Nepal
Current City: Atlanta, GA

> "IF I LOOK BACK IN MY COUNTRY, MY FUTURE WOULD NOT BE BRIGHT. IN THE REFUGEE CAMP, I WOULD HAVE TO WORK THE SAME AS THE OTHERS. IF YOU ARE EDUCATED, OR IF YOU ARE NOT EDUCATED, YOU HAVE TO WORK THE SAME KIND OF WORK."

I was born in Pokhara, then we moved to the Timai camp. In the camp, at that time, I was so small that I didn't know it was hard for me or that it was difficult for me. I know now it was hard for my parents, and it was hard for my family.

When I became a six-year-old, I started school. School was made of bamboo, like camp. I started my school, and my dad decided to go work because we didn't have enough money for food, clothes, and other stuff like that. Each year he came back and gave us money for the house, our clothes, and for others. For a few years he did not come back, so my mother decided to go find him. She couldn't find him, and she came back to the camp. She told my uncle, and my uncle decided to go find him. He went to the mid-east of Pokhara, Nepal, but he couldn't find him. My dad never came back. He left us.

There was a UN person who helped us. They provided food, education, and shelter, like houses for homeless people who got kicked out from their countries. One day, the Timai camp was emptied because the people went to the US, and the UN decided to move people in that camp to another camp. We had to follow the rules of the UN because if we didn't follow the rules, we could be homeless. We followed the rules of the UN, and we moved to the Beldangi Refugee Camp. It was the same, like Timai.

Then, we started school. I started from fourth grade, and my brother started from third grade. My mother took care of us. My grandparents used to work in a farm there in the Timai Village. They sent us money because my mom couldn't work. She has a kind of sickness. They'd send us money each year and each month for home stuff.

One day, my uncle decided to go to the US. He applied for his process, and he went to the US. After a few months, he called us and he said to us, "The US is better than camp. Your child would have a better future in the US, so you could come here." Then, my mom decided to go to the US, and my uncle helped her in her process.

For all of us to go, they needed my dad. It was a few years, and they said, "Get your dad's lost form to have his signature." We did not find my father, but one day my uncle got his death form. The hospital gave us the death form in India. We were given the document for his signature in order to come to the United States.

We handled it with the IOM. They said, "You have to go, and you can wait for your process." They called us for a medical checkup, and then they taught us. We had orientation in camp, and they taught us how to go to the restroom, and if you need help in the US you need to call 911. If somebody is going to do something bad, like a stranger, you have to call 911. If you don't know English, just hold the phone for some seconds and then they are going to transfer your phone. They also taught you what you were going to do in a plane: how you need food, how to ask for help, and stuff like that. If you wanted to change your seat, you have to ask the other people.

Then we had a flight from Jhapa to Kathmandu. We stayed in Kathmandu for ten days. The IOM provided for the refugee people with a hostel, and we stayed there. From there we had a flight from Kathmandu to Qatar, and we stayed eight hours there. We went from Qatar to Miami, Florida and from Miami to Atlanta.

When I came from Florida to Atlanta, I was kind of nervous because my health was kind of like a sickness. In the plane, we did not rest well, so I was kind of sick. We saw our case manager, my uncle, aunt, and our cousins. They were waiting for us in the airport. My mother was crying because she missed her mother and father. They are too old, and they can't work. I was kind of nervous on how to find my uncle and aunt. I was scared that maybe we were going to get lost. After we were on the airplane for two hours, I saw my uncle. My family was calling me, and I was so excited to see them. They hugged me and were like, "How was your journey?" I said, "It was not bad, but I was kind of nervous in the plane," because that was my first time in a plane. My mom was still crying. She missed her mother and father.

The first week in the US was not bad. We met all our relatives, and we had fun. My uncle threw us a party, and my family called the church people. When they arrived, they prayed for us, and they prayed for our better future and better life. We had a lot of fun. We went to a picnic in Stone Mountain with our parents, relatives, and my uncle. It was really amazing.

School in the US is different than my country's school. It is so amazing. The school is so big. I thought, if I go in, I will be lost. The first week of school I was kind of nervous, but we had a Nepali interpreter there telling me everything: how to get food and how to get lunch in the cafeteria, and I got a student lunch number. The first day of school I was not talking with people yet because I was shy. I already knew of a few English words, but I'm shy to speak. I stayed quiet the first day. I didn't make friends. At school, it is now better. There are some people who speak my language, so I talk with them. We have a good time in and out of school. The teachers help us too. If you don't know English, they help you by their actions.

If I look back in my country, my future would not be bright. In the refugee camp, I would have to work the same as the others. If you are educated, or if you are not educated, you have to work the same kind of work. You have to carry heavy things and build construction. My future would not be much because we are not citizens of Nepal. The government does not accept us in Nepal because my mother and grandmother are from Bhutan, and they got kicked out of their country. I don't know what happened in Bhutan, but the Bhutanese government kicked them out of their country into a Nepal camp.

Life is different here than in camp. The camp was terrible for me, but here I can learn. I will learn so many things I cannot learn in Nepal. If I learn, and if I do more and more, I will get a better future here in Atlanta. I will get a better job, I hope. After five years, we will be citizens of the US.

I love to play soccer, and my favorite subject is social studies. I love historical things and learning about more historical things of the world. On the weekend, I learn about the history of countries. I hope I will be an engineer in the United States. I love to do technical things and make things.

When I think about my future, I don't know everything about it. I have one dream: to make my mom proud of me. I'm the biggest one in my family, so I have to do everything for them. When I grow up, I hope I will get a better job. I will help my mom and help my family.

VIDEO LINKS

greencardvoices.org/speakers/sanjith-yadav

Illustration by Yehimi Cambrón

America

From: Tampico, Mexico
Current City: Atlanta, GA

"I KNOW WHAT IT'S LIKE TO FEEL LIKE YOU DON'T HAVE ANY RIGHTS AND TO FEEL LIKE YOU DON'T BELONG AND TO FEEL INJUSTICE. I REALLY WANT TO MAKE A CHANGE. I WANT TO HELP PEOPLE THAT FEEL LIKE THEY DON'T HAVE A VOICE BECAUSE THEY DO HAVE A VOICE."

I was born in Tampico, Mexico. I lived with my mom and my dad for two months when I was born, but then my dad came to the United States and so I only lived with my mom. We lived with my grandparents because she couldn't take care of me on her own. Eventually we moved. We rented a house only for me and my mom, and then when we were going to come back to the United States, we moved back with my grandpa and my grandma. My grandpa was my father figure because I didn't have my dad. He was the person that I called dad.

My mom said that it was really hard for her to take care of me because she couldn't move around. She didn't have any means of transportation, so whenever I would get sick, it was really hard for her to take me to the hospital. She was not planning on being a single mother and so life was really hard, but she did her best to make it as best as it could be for me.

I was two years old when I came to the United States. I was told that when my dad tried to hold me I cried because I didn't know who he was and that really hurt him. So it was just painful for him that I did not recognize him and did not have that connection right away. I remember we lived in a small apartment, but then we moved into a bigger apartment. In that apartment I lived with fifteen people. They were not all family members, but some of them were friends of my family. It was just that they were all barely arriving to the United States, and we decided to all live together to pay the rent together so it wouldn't be so hard. So my mom, my dad, me, and my brother shared a room, and then everybody else there found where to stay inside the apartment. It was very hard to live with a lot of people because it was very crowded and noisy all the time, but I liked having all my uncles around because now I don't. I just have a few of them so I kind of miss that.

When I started school no one around me knew how to speak English, and so it was very hard. But my mom found a way to teach me English even though she did not know the language herself, and because of her, I wasn't placed in any ESOL classes. I was able to continue school learning English, but there was a conflict because when I was in Pre-K, my teachers knew Spanish and would speak to me in Spanish. My mom would get really mad because I wasn't learning any English. So she had to try harder to teach me English.

Now I live in an apartment with only my mom, my brother, and my dad. My dad has come a long way. When he got here, he started cleaning restaurants at night with a company, and now he has his own company cleaning restaurants. He's an employer, and I am very proud of him because of that. I'm the person that helps my mom out with chores and with cooking and taking care of my brother.

My favorite subject at school is social studies. I just love learning about anything like history, economics, and all of that. My hobbies that I really like are cooking and baking. I also like reading and spending time with my family.

In the future, I hope to either become an activist or a civil rights attorney because I know what it's like to feel like you don't have any rights and to feel like you don't belong and to feel injustice. I really want to make a change. I want to help people that feel like they don't have a voice because they do have a voice. I want to help them because I've been around people like that, and I am someone like that myself. I want to make a change.

When we came to the United States, we had to leave behind all of my family, so I only have a little bit of family here. It's all from my dad's side. I don't know anyone from my mom's side. Two years ago, my grandpa passed away and it was really hard because I never got to meet him. My dad didn't see his father for fifteen years before he passed away, and I can't imagine not seeing my father and then losing him. It just makes me sad because of the way the country is right now, I don't get the opportunity to see my family. That's another reason I want to make a difference—I don't want anyone else to go through this. It just make me really sad that my parents left behind so many things, like all of their family, to come to a country where we're not welcomed, and that's just really hard for me.

When I think about freedom, I think about the ability to, you know, have just basic human rights. Freedom is, or should be, a basic human right.

I think that freedom should be having the ability to go back to your country because you leave a lot behind but know that you can come back. I miss my country and the people that we left behind, but I know that the conditions are really terrible and that it's not safe. I would like to go to meet all the people that we left behind and get to see what my country is like.

My parents were the original Dreamers because they came to this country in search of the American Dream. Like I said, they left everything behind because in their minds this country was everything for them. It was new jobs and more opportunities. It was escaping dangerous conditions. It was escaping poverty in our home country, and it was giving their children the opportunities that they couldn't have. My parents weren't even able to reach high school, so for them to see me being a senior and graduating in a few months is showing them that all their sacrifices were worth something.

The American Dream is what keeps me motivated to do good things and to just become someone in life. My dad wasn't able to see his father for fifteen years, and we weren't able to see him or be there when he was dying. He wasn't even able to go to his father's grave. Because of the American Dream, he gave all of that up for me. So the American Dream is my motivation to keep going for my parents.

VIDEO LINKS

greencardvoices.org/speakers/america

Adama, Ethiopia

Eliyas Sala

From: Adama, Ethiopia
Current City: Atlanta, GA

> "FOR ME, THE AMERICAN DREAM IS PURSUING YOUR PASSION AND TRYING TO BE THAT PERSON YOU HAVE ALWAYS DREAMT OF BECOMING."

I remember a lot about Ethiopia because I came here just five years ago, and I lived most of my life there. I was born in Adama, or some people call it Nazret, Ethiopia. It is the second main city of Ethiopia. Ethiopia is kind of an underdeveloped world, populated by men and women who live as herders. I had a lot of friends, relatives, and families there. My cousins, aunts, and uncles all lived in our same community, and my grandma lived with me and my family. I also remember playing with my friends. We used to do a lot of playing soccer.

Me and my younger brother were actually enrolled in a public school in Ethiopia, and when I was there, a lot of people wore torn clothing, like torn uniforms. Students would have to bring their lunches, usually containing different ethnic foods, and we would all eat in the classroom. There were a lot of students per class, about forty, and they were all various ages. A lot of the students were in their thirties. Unlike here, where teachers use electronic boards, we used chalk and board. I remember being asked to demonstrate something in class, and it was hard for me to transfer between chalkboards and the Promethean Boards here. The public schools here look like universities. I saw Promethean Boards and projectors being regularly utilized by students.

One day, eight years ago, my parents took us to some place where we entered the Green Card lottery, or the Diversity Immigrant Visa Program. Basically that means a lot of families try and put in their information to get the chance to come here. Their application is reviewed, and then they are chosen. Last time I checked, the chances of coming here were very low. For the whole world, 50,000 people get it out of 19 million per year.

Our whole family applied, and only my father got it. He could have taken all of us, but since my parents were not able to afford it all, they went first. When my parents told us about our opportunity, a lot of my relatives were talking about it. Believe it or not, the whole town was talking about it. A lot of people offered my parents money to buy their lottery tickets to get the chance to come to America. Me and my brother did not know what the lottery meant at the time, but we knew it was some kind of miracle. We were very fortunate.

When both of my parents left, we lived with our grandma. I was filled with very complex emotions. I just remember really wanting to go with them. There were a lot of times where we missed our parents. There were times it actually felt like we got used to not having parents at all, and that was very weird. My brother and I had a stronger bond while we lived in Ethiopia because we needed each other's support. My parents were in America for three years without us.

When they were here in America, they were settling and getting financially stable. My parents would call us every day just to hear our voices, and whenever they called, I remember getting really happy. We talked about their expectations of me once I arrived in America. One day, almost four years after my parents left, my mom and my dad called us, and they told me and my brother that we were going to come to America. I couldn't really believe it. I thought I was dreaming. After so many years, it felt like it was too good to be true. I was asking my grandma just to say it again, one more time. One thing I really remember is that I thought once we got our tickets, I wasn't going to be able to see them. I thought that maybe by some kind of unfortunate incident I might not be able to go to America because I couldn't believe it.

I remember at the airport in Ethiopia, I was waiting for my mom to come back from America. It had been years, and I could not recognize her face. She had a different hairstyle. It felt like she was a stranger. Looking back now, it was confusing. I recalled some of her distinctive features, and then it took me back to the time when I was waving my hands saying goodbye at that same airport. We were both filled with so much emotion.

The journey from Ethiopia to America was long, tiring, and exhausting. We took two airplanes: first, we went to Frankfurt, Germany, and then we came to Atlanta. I hated the airplane food. It had a strange taste. When I first came here, I went straight to the International Center, here in Atlanta, so I could learn. Even when I was at the International Center, I was at a disadvantage compared to other people. Most of them came from South and Central American countries, which are different but similar because they speak Spanish. Believe it or not, it was only me and my brother in that International Center from Eastern Africa. I remember a lot of people speaking English, and I did not understand a single word.

In Ethiopia, my father was an English and language arts teacher, so we knew a little bit of English. He didn't want us to struggle with our English in America, so he asked me and my brother to bring dictionaries back with us. In Ethiopia, if someone actually spoke English, it would indicate that that person has a high level of status, and my father wanted that for us. When we came here, my dad told us many times, even like every day as a reminder, that he wanted us to go to the best schools like Harvard or other Ivy League schools. Someone like my father having such high expectations of us succeeding at that level and me not being able to understand or communicate was very disturbing and emotionally stressing. I felt like I was never going to be able to speak English. It felt like I was on some other planet.

Me and my brother were minorities in the International Center. They only had Spanish-English dictionaries, so I understood why my dad wanted us to bring our own. I had to do a lot of memorization of basic words, watch a lot of videos, and learn grammar rules, but my father helped us by testing our vocabulary each week. After years of hard work and learning, and after having a lot of great teachers who believed in me, I now speak better English. I was in eighth grade when we came here, and school was not good. Making friends was hard, and I never really talked to other people. But when I came to Cross Keys High School, it was much better. I was surrounded by similar peers. I have achieved and been through a lot. I love it here.

Before, in the movies, I have seen America portrayed as a place like a heaven. Don't get me wrong, America is a lot better than where I used to live, but I guess I dreamt of that place because I desperately needed that place. However, I failed to consider the possibility that there were going to be lots of challenges here. Speaking and being able to understand English was overwhelming and really, really difficult at first. Learning the language was one of the hardest challenges I faced, but knowing English is a must in order to advance in society.

For me, the American Dream is pursuing your passion and trying to be that person you have always dreamt of becoming. My passion is being able to help others, and my vision is to become a math professor and fulfill my college goals. I am very, very passionate about math because, compared to other subjects, it did not really require lots of knowledge of English. I liked working with numbers better than words. Math helped me come out of my shell.

If I had not come to America, I would have a different identity. Before I came here, I liked school, but education was just not exactly a priority over there. I did not feel passionate about school and learning. Now my passion is learning. There are so many great resources here. I am pretty sure if I had stayed in Ethiopia I would be working some pretty laborious jobs, and there would be less of a chance I would actually go to college. For the first two years of college, I want to go to a school in Georgia, like Georgia State, and then transfer to an Ivy League school. I want to meet my dad's expectations and do well in school because it feels good to succeed.

If I could give advice, I would just tell someone in my same situation that everything is okay, and I would mean it. I wish someone had given me the impression that they meant it when they said it. The entire journey from Ethiopia and America was fortunate. This all happened because of a lottery ticket, and we are so lucky to be here.

VIDEO LINKS

greencardvoices.org/speakers/eliyas-sala

Chin Matupi,
Myanmar

May Da

From: Chin Matupi, Myanmar
Current City: Atlanta, GA

"I WANTED TO GO TO THE US FASTER. I DON'T WANT TO STAY LONGER IN MALAYSIA BECAUSE THERE WAS A LOT OF POLICE TRYING TO CATCH BURMESE PEOPLE . . . AND I WAS SO SCARED OF THAT. I KEEP PRAYING TO GOD TO LET ME GO TO THE U.S."

I was born in Chin Matupi. When I was seven years old, my dad went to Malaysia. I was living with my mom and my grandparents for almost eight years. I went to a hospital one week. When I came back from the hospital, I looked for my grandfather, but I couldn't find him. I asked my mom and she did not answer me, but she was upset when I asked my brother. She said my grandpa ran away. I asked why, and she said it was because of the army. I always feel upset about that. My uncle ran to my house and told my mom the army was in our grandparents' house. They caught my grandma, and she went to jail. After she came back in 2010, my grandpa called my grandma to come to India, and they all went.

I stayed with my mom and my great-grandfather. My father called us to come to Malaysia. I was so upset, and I didn't want to leave my great-grandfather because he was alone in my village, and my mom also did not want to leave. My mom said she didn't want to go to Malaysia because my great-grandpa was still in Myanmar, so my mom said, "Just give me a chance to think about that." Later my mom called my father back. She said, "We will come to Malaysia." My mom was thinking about the future for me and my brother because if we stayed in Myanmar we couldn't go to school any longer, so that was really difficult for us.

When I was twelve years old, I went to Malaysia, and on the first day at refugee camp school, I was so nervous. I had never seen so many different people before, and my father told me to go to school. I couldn't even write English and couldn't speak it. I didn't know anything, so I went to school. Everybody was speaking English, and they talked to me. Some people bullied me, so I was crying. The kids there made fun of me because I couldn't under-stand English. Every day I was crying in class, so I did not talk to anybody. It was a lot of all of the same people there. The school's name is ACR: Alliance of Chin Refugees. Kids in school were Burmese, but teachers and students were supposed to speak English. We just talk in Burmese. We were learning about science in English and geography in English. So in 2013, I felt better because I had friends now, and I could speak a little in English. I was so happy. Now I wanna go back to see my friends. I still miss them.

When I was fifteen, my mom told me we had to go to the US. She said, "If you wanna work, you can work." We didn't have that much money. If we went to the US, we would need a lot of money. We had to buy a lot of stuff. So, I was working for one year and a half at a clothes shop outside the refugee camp. I didn't go to school when I was working. I was so nervous, and I was trying my best to talk like normal. I sent money to my grandparents.

Later the UN called us to check our blood, so we went to the UN to get it checked. They said, "We will call you back if you got a pass or a fail," so we were waiting for the phone call. One week later they called us, and they said my older brother had TB. So we had to stay there for six months before entering the US. My brother took medicine for six months for TB. I was so upset because I wanted to go to the US faster. I didn't want to stay longer in Malaysia because there was a lot of police trying to catch Burmese people who were working outside the refugee camp, and I was so scared of that. I kept praying to God to let me go to the US. I wanted to study more. I wanted to go to school. So, I kept praying, but we could not do anything. So I just kept working. In 2016 they called us and told us, "You guys passed." July 27th, they said we could go, so I was so happy. My brother and my family were so happy. I was also worried about moving. I still feel better than the first time we came, but I was so nervous. This place is so different from Malaysia.

The first day here in the US, my uncle told me, "Don't go outside. There are a lot of strangers, and they're gonna catch you." So I just stayed at home. I did not open the door. I just stayed in the room. So because at this time it was night in Malaysia, I was sleeping. I was sleeping when everybody was there at my house, but I did not talk with them. At night I was awake and talked to my brother. My mom was so angry because they were trying to sleep. At night we were awake and in the day we slept.

My house in Malaysia was really different from here because in Malaysia we have just an open space. It had no bedrooms, just a living room. We were living with six people there. My auntie was living with us too, so seven people were sleeping in the living room together. There were no bedrooms, no kitchen. There was just one room. We had no place to put our chairs. Here we have three bedrooms, two bathrooms, and a living room. I was so happy we had a kitchen and a dining room. If my friends came to my house, we could sit in the living room and have fun. It's really different.

In Malaysia, we had to cook by ourselves at home and bring food to school. We were eating our own food at school. Here, we do not bring anything, just a bag, and we go to school, and we eat breakfast and lunch. That's really different from Malaysia. On the first day of school, I felt it was okay and I didn't feel nervous this time, but I was still nervous to talk to the teacher. Now everything is okay. I have been here about one year and a half. My favorite subjects are English and math, and I really like dancing. If my parents told me to go back to Myanmar, I would because I still want to see my grandparents. My dad really wants me to be a nurse, and I want to make him happy.

VIDEO LINKS

greencardvoices.org/speakers/may-da

Illustration by Yehimi Cambrón

Karelin

From: Petén, Guatemala
Current City: Atlanta, GA

> "I SEE THAT THERE ARE A LOT OF DISADVANTAGES IN MINORITY COMMUNITIES,
> ESPECIALLY FOR LATINOS, SO I WANT TO GO TO COLLEGE AND STUDY IN A FIELD WHERE
> I CAN HELP MY COMMUNITY, LIKE PUBLIC HEALTH OR INTERNATIONAL RELATIONS."

I was born in the northern part of Guatemala in the department of Petén, which is the equivalent of a state or a province. I lived in a really small town called Tierra Blanca, which translates to "white sand" or "white dirt." As far as I can remember, when I was in Guatemala, I lived with my aunt because my mother came to the US when I was really young. I remember having a carefree life, playing freeze tag with my cousins, climbing trees, or just running around barefoot. My aunt has two daughters that are within my age range, so I spent most of my free time with them, and we got along very well. It was a really fun, carefree life. Tierra Blanca is a really small town, so there were few houses with electricity or running water. Having that was a luxury, so coming to the US was a big change.

I have four siblings total: two older sisters, an older brother, and a younger half-brother from my mom's side. My mom came to the US when I was only two, but she returned to Guatemala five years later to bring one of my older sisters and me to the US. Three or four years ago, my older brother came to the US. Now basically the whole family is here, including uncles, aunts, and cousins. My older sister decided to stay in Guatemala when my mom went to get us because she was close to graduating from high school. She is a nurse now.

I get along with my siblings well. Right now, I only live with my mom and my brother, who is thirteen and annoying and frustrating, but I still love him. My older siblings are more like parental figures; they provide a lot of guidance and support in my education. Family is a big part of my life because, as a Latina, it is engrained in my culture.

I just remember being confused when my mom returned to Guatemala because I felt like I didn't know her. Being two, you don't have very many clear memories, so I did not remember her as being my mother. I actually denied her as my mom. It was as if she was a complete stranger. Then, I was suddenly told that I was going to the US with a strange woman; it was a big shock. I knew her through pictures, but there were no clear memories to create an intimate connection. I remember being very rude to her and refusing to hug her or even get close to her. Now my relationship with my mom is very different. We are really close. She is really supportive with my education, and I confide everything in her. I am grateful that she brought me to the US where I can have an opportunity at higher education.

In coming to the US, I had to give up my family. The person who I cared for the most was my grandfather. He played the role of a paternal figure in my life because I did not grow up with my father, and many of the good memories I have in Guatemala involve him. He always protected me and instructed me in doing the right thing. He sparked my love for reading and education because even though he had never formally attended school, he had taught himself how to read. He would read me amazing legends of the Maya and our culture and heritage. He passed away a while back, but he would usually come visit us over the summer, and it was always a joy to see him.

Most of the contact that I have with my family in Guatemala is through my mom. She speaks on the phone to my aunts and uncles, and they send her pictures of the family. The only two people that I would speak to directly were my granddad before he passed away and my older sister.

When I first arrived in the US, I had to stay with my uncle and his wife because my sister, my mom, and my aunt had not yet arrived. I remember the day that they were coming home. I had no idea that they would be there. My uncle's wife told me to get dressed and wear something nice, and I remember saying, "Oh, it's not like the president is coming to visit."

For the majority of my life since coming to the US, I lived in a small town called Glennville that is about an hour away from Savannah, Georgia. I went to Glennville Elementary and Middle School. Living there was not much of a change. In terms of commodities, the living situation, and the language barrier it was different, but the scenery was very much like my hometown. There were expansive fields of corn and a lot of nature and trees. It was a familiar setting that I liked.

My first day of school was definitely different. I remember I rode the bus to school. At the time, the middle school students shared the bus with the elementary school children. It was such a small town that the county could do that. On the way to school my sister kept asking me to repeat my room number and asking me how I would get around, so that I wouldn't get lost. I was so shy and confused that she had to approach a student on the bus that looked around my age and ask her if she could guide me to the English as a second language teacher's office.

When I was finally taken to my class, I found out that the same girl from the bus was in the same class with me. Her name was Zaira, and she quickly became my best friend over the years. She would translate for me and help me with my work. It really helped that I had someone like her in a school that was for the most part filled with White students. Having her as a friend eased the transition for me. Learning English was hard at first, but being so young, I picked it up within a few months. I was in the same class with Zaira for only the first grade because my performance in school improved so much that I was introduced to the advanced classes while she stayed behind.

Growing up, I would get called stuck up or snobby because I was in advanced classes, and there was this stereotype against people talking or acting like a White person. I felt conflicted because when I first came here, I was a little Latina girl who could not even speak English, and now, I was getting backlash from my own Latino community for just being myself. It was definitely hard for me at that time.

The summer before eighth grade, my family decided to move to South Carolina because of financial and work reasons. My mom is a single mom, so she has had to move around a lot in search of jobs to help sustain my brother and me. When I arrived in South Carolina, we moved into a small home in Charleston, which is an area that is very much split among the races. There is a lot gerrymandering in the school system, so most people of color, Blacks and Hispanics, had to go to the same underfunded school, while most other White children had huge remodeled state of the art buildings. There was a big difference in the education system.

At the end of my eighth grade year, I applied to a magnet school, which was predominantly White. I do not look Hispanic, so I mixed in with the crowd. At that time, I buried myself in my studies, and I kind of shut down on the rest of the world because I felt very different in terms of social class and education. I had to take public transportation to get to and from school, even though the school was only fifteen minutes away from my house. Most of the students rode the school bus from the surrounding islands that were thirty minutes away. It felt really unfair to me. I could not get a school bus because I was the only student from my area. Most kids from those poor neighborhoods did not get accepted into the magnet program. Even though it was a hard time in my life, it was definitely a good learning experience for me. I learned to treasure my differences and to fight for what matters to me; education is really important to me.

At the beginning of my sophomore year, I moved to Atlanta for the same financial reasons. I am really glad to have moved to Atlanta because it has opened more doors to many wonderful opportunities. Before I came here, I didn't think much about going to college. I always knew that I wanted to pursue higher education, but I didn't know what being an immigrant would entail. Of course I knew there were barriers, but I didn't know how to navigate those barriers. There are a lot of supportive people here to talk to about college, and they teach us about different ways to apply to college as an immigrant student. Considering my situation, I am glad to have moved here. When I came to Cross Keys, there was definitely a cultural shock. Even though I am Latino, I had never seen so many people like myself in one place. It was a very welcoming experience. Atlanta is such a big and welcoming city, so I have many opportunities that I did not have in Charleston, much less in Glennville. I did an internship with Emory and Grady; I pushed myself to pursue more challenging courses, and I applied to QuestBridge. I have applied to so many programs that I did not even know existed.

My friends and I would probably fall into the nerd category. They are very into math and outgoing in terms of academics. My other friends are also very relaxed and into designing things, like robots and programming. They are great people.

I see that there are a lot of disadvantages in minority communities, especially for Latinos, so I want to go to college and study in a field where I can help my community, like public health or international relations. My goals are ambitious but definitely attainable. I applied to many colleges through QuestBridge. QuestBridge is an organization that helps low-income, high-achieving students in their quest to being accepted to top universities; they basically breach the socio-economic barrier. I have applied to a lot of universities, but my top college is Yale. Of course, that is a reach school, but hopefully I will be accepted. I'm not exactly sure what I want to do just yet, but I want to help my community in some way. I want to help people like myself. Right now, I am thinking of international relations or political science because I want to help people in my situation and because I have a really strong background with languages. I really like languages.

When I think of the American Dream, I think of people being able to overcome adversity to fulfill their dreams. For me, it is about being able to pursue an education, to attend college, and to be able to use those skills you have learned as a way of helping my community. I think that even though the American Dream is good, it is still very idealized. You come to the US and you work hard in the hopes that you will achieve your goals with more resources or more ease than most other countries. A lot of people in our home country do not think of the struggles that most of us have to go through to live in this country.

I think democracy is when people are able to take action and voice their thoughts for issues that they feel strongly about without being shut down or discriminated against. It is the idea of being able to have real influence over government figures that make decisions, which affect our daily lives. When I think of freedom, I think of the textbook definition that we are taught in school—the freedom to be able to voice your thoughts and beliefs without discrimination.

I have seen it in my mom. She has had to work backbreaking jobs just to get by, pay the rent, and put us through school. That is something that a lot of people do not see. Before I was even born, my dad left my mom for another woman, and she has had to work hard to give us the best she can afford. My mom is a strong woman and I have learned a lot about perseverance and determination from her. She is one of the most influential and inspiring people in my life.

VIDEO LINKS

greencardvoices.org/speakers/karelin

Addis Ababa,
Ethiopia

Faysal Ando

From: Addis Ababa, Ethiopia
Current City: Atlanta, GA

"THE ONLY THING THAT'S HARD FOR ME IS TRYING TO REMEMBER THE THINGS FROM BEFORE. TRYING TO STILL KEEP THAT PART OF ME—MY CULTURE AND MY COUNTRY."

Before I was born, my parents moved to Saudi Arabia. My dad had a job as a taxi driver, and my mom worked cleaning people's houses. We used to live near my aunt who also lived in Saudi Arabia. When I was born, me and my mom had the chance to go to America. We got the visa—the DV. We got the chance to go to America, but my dad could not go to America. My dad went to Ethiopia because we had all our family in Ethiopia.

In 2002, me and my mom went to America. I do not even remember very much because I was two years old. Then we went to Ethiopia to see my dad. At that point, I stayed in Ethiopia, and my mom went back to America. I did not see my mom for a good six years, I think. We were separated, so it was hard because I could only be with one parent. Me, my dad, and the rest of the family lived in Ethiopia. The only people we knew in America were my uncle and my mom, so we stayed in Ethiopia. I did not really see my dad. He would go to the city to work. I pretty much lived with my aunt and uncle.

The things I remember from Ethiopia are that I used to have this brother, but he really wasn't my brother. He was not my brother by blood, but he used to live with us, so he was like my brother to me and that is what I called him. I remember playing soccer on the streets—there were no streets actually. It was just dirt. I was a child when I got my first soccer ball. Me and my brother would play soccer every day after that; it's just what we did all day. My mom and dad's families lived in separate areas. We lived close to the city. The school was near, but it was hard to get to because there was this big cliff. My aunt would take me every day. It was not a long walk, but it was a very big cliff; you had to climb down and then climb back up to get to the other side. I remember my aunt would take me at twelve o'clock every day to school. We used to see hyenas and stuff too.

When I first found out that I was going to come to America, it was maybe a few weeks before we actually left, so we did not have much time to adjust. I barely had time to say bye to most of the people that I knew. It was kind of hard on me, but I was really excited at the same time to go to a different country with better education and better jobs, stuff like that. I remember at the airport the whole family came. There was this big transparent screen, and me and my father were going to the plane, and we could see everyone crying. I will forever have this image in my mind. If I ever need motivation or a drive to become better, I think of this moment.

So in 2008, me and my dad went together to America to finally be with my mom. I was eight or nine. We had not seen her in a very long time. I did not even remember her face. The plane ride was nice to me. I didn't have any problems even though it was only my second time on a plane. It was almost a direct flight. We made one or two stops; we stopped in Washington, DC. Then we got on a flight to come to Atlanta.

Once we got to America, I did not recognize my mom at all. I had not seen her in so long, so I was like, "Who's that?" and then they told me, "That's your mom." That was a really sad moment for me to know that I had gotten to a point in my childhood where I did not even recognize my own mother. It really felt like I had not seen her in forever. We went into my house; I still live there. We live in a condo, and my first apartment was two rooms and two bathrooms. We had to move down a level because I used to make way too much noise up top and the people downstairs had a problem with that. So we had to switch to a different apartment.

When I first came to America, I was surprised because I thought it would be all a big city and big buildings, but in Atlanta, there are a bunch of trees. It looked like a forest to me, and I thought it was going to be a bunch of buildings. There were buildings, and that was confusing to me. The first few weeks of school I started in the second grade because I went to kindergarten and first grade in Ethiopia.

I remember this one time I was trying to ask the teacher for tissues, but I didn't know what the English word for tissues was at the time, so my nose was runny the whole time. I had no idea what to say, and I was just sitting there. I tried to communicate with her, but we could not. I just got up and took a tissue from the box. That was the only thing I could do. It was really hard because we had education in Ethiopia where my aunt used to take me, but they didn't know much. So when I came here, I didn't know much.

They taught English, but it was not advanced like the English they teach here in the US. It was really strict there in Ethiopia. The teachers were allowed to hit you and stuff if they wanted, so that was hard for me as a student there.

I have two brothers. They were born in 2009 and 2010. I started making friends. I usually make lots of friends; I do not really have a problem with that. I made my friends, and I still have them to this day. There were only a few things that were the same to me between Ethiopia and the US. Everything else was different. So many cars, so many other stuff, but the people were nice to me here and there. The one thing I still remember that is the same is that I played soccer in Ethiopia, and I still play soccer here. That has helped me make friends and adapt to the new environment. Soccer is one of those things that is the same all over the world. You can go anywhere, and it will not change. It is a constant thing you can find everywhere that helps you assimilate with new people and adjust to a new life.

Once I started making friends, living here became much easier for me. At first I felt like the only Muslim here. There are a few Muslims here and we are friends, but most of my friends are Christians. It is different for me because I cannot do all the things they do like eating pork and stuff like that. I do not have it that bad here, but I know other people go through hardships. The media focuses on the bad. Every religion has bad people, but the media chooses the worst things to talk about when it comes to Islam. I feel like people are constantly bombarded with depressing or angry ideas that only make the people watching the news have a bad understanding of who we really are.

In America, it was not that hard for me because I adapted really quickly. The only thing that's hard for me is trying to remember the things from before, trying to still keep that part of me—my culture and my country. My family speaks Amharic. I know how to speak it, but I became illiterate in it. Hanging on to that stuff can be hard when you come to the US and learn about a whole different culture and country.

I am in the eleventh grade at Cross Keys, and I'm a secretary for my grade. One of the things I enjoy doing other than soccer is to read. I read a lot. That really helped me further understand my English. I do not like nonfiction books, but I will read almost any book I can get my hands on. Probably my favorite book of all time is *Slaughterhouse Five*. It is a really good book. I read *The Catcher in the Rye*. Those are some of the best books I have ever read. I play soccer for the school and club, so that really helped me make friends. I play on the junior varsity soccer team. These are just some of the ways I meet other people, learn more about the language, and learn more about the culture.

I am not sure what I want to do in the future. I know I am going to college. That is just a must. I am probably going to be the first one in my family going to college, so I really want to help my family because I have got this chance. They want me to become something and not go through all the work they went through. If I am able to get into a team, I may play soccer. I do not know yet what I want to major in. I do think about doing something in psychology, or maybe engineering.

Once I get that down and choose the path I want, I plan to become successful and make a good amount of money, and then hopefully send it back to my country because I still have my brother there. I want to help him out. I want to help my aunts out and everyone else who is still there. It is really hard for people over there right now. I mean I would love to have them come here, but that is not really a choice right now because it is really hard to let people come into this country.

My mom and dad have gone back to Ethiopia a few times. Someday I want to go back there to visit my family and discover more about my country. I would like to make money to help my family out because I feel like I got very lucky by coming here. It is a lot of pressure to help them because I am the only one that got this chance to get this far. We call our family every once in a while, so we keep in touch with them. We send money back home to Ethiopia, to their parents. We still have to help them. When you move, you still have past connections, and you still have to help them out.

I think life would have been harder in Ethiopia because recently there have been tensions between cultures like Oromo. Not that many people know about Ethiopia. There are political struggles right now. Christians, Muslims, there are lots of fights, and the government is corrupt. That would have been hard. Not as bad as some other people have it, but it would have been hard. I would have had to go to school because that is a big thing in my family, but I do not know if I would have gotten the same level of education. I would not have seen most of the things I have seen today, and I would not know as much. But still, it is not as bad over there as people think. It is a struggle, but most of the bad things that people think happen in Africa are not actually true. There are buildings, TVs, cars, and other things people would normally find here in the US. It is not exactly like the US, but it still is not that bad. We have our struggles, but there are still things there that most people in the US do not know about.

I am not really sure if the American Dream is true or not anymore because for some people it is because you become successful, but it is really hard now for others to do the same. There are so many bad things happening especially here, like with DACA and all that stopping so many people from reaching the American Dream, which is being successful, coming to America as an immigrant, and making it farther in life than you would have in your old country. But all of that is not possible if they are kicking people out of the country for pretty much no reason. Some days I wonder if things will ever be fair or if corruption will ever stop.

For my parents, success is not having to worry about anything in your life really. Money for things like a good car, a job, spending time with your family, and sustaining a house. For me, it is somewhat that and taking care of my family. Taking care of my family is super important to me. The idea of helping my family and making sure they do not have anything to worry about is a big driving force in my life. They motivate me to do more, and I want to do more for them. I want to be happy. Right now, I do not have a definition for success. I am still trying to figure it out for myself, but whatever it is, I know I will be successful.

VIDEO LINKS

greencardvoices.org/speakers/faysal-ando

Michoacán,
Mexico

Illustration by Yehimi Cambrón

Yehimi Cambrón

From: Michoacán, Mexico
Current City: Atlanta, GA

"I'M DOING EVERYTHING I CAN . . . . TO MAKE SURE THAT MY ACTIONS ARE ACTIONS OF PERMANENCY AND TO PAINT MURALS THAT WILL BE HERE FOREVER EVEN IF I'M NOT. TO TOUCH THE LIVES OF MY STUDENTS AND PLANT SEEDS THAT WILL ALWAYS BLOOM HERE."

I didn't spend much time in Mexico. I was there for seven years. One thing that I remember a lot are the houses that we lived in and my dad not being there most of the time. Each time my dad ran out of work, he would always cross the border and come work here. My mom pretty much raised us on her own. Every time one of us was born, my dad would migrate here, cross the border and work here. He'd work jobs like working in the kitchens of Chinese restaurants. He did that for years. Maybe like ten, fifteen years? But I had a lot of resentment towards my dad because of that, because he was never there when we were in Mexico.

We were really poor, and I didn't understand how my dad spent so much time working here to send money back home, yet we were still living in poverty. Because I have DACA, I was able to go back and visit two summers ago through Advance Parole, and I visited the house that we lived in. Being in our house again, I had this huge realization that the reason my dad was always here working was because he was sending money back to build the houses we called home.

It kind of reminds me of the story of the three little pigs because our first house that we had was built from a material called lamina, and so I just remember—every time it rained—my mom would put pots and pans all over the floor to catch water. So that was our first house. The second house my dad built when he came back from working in the US was a house made out of wood. So it was a little bit stronger and provided more protection. The third time he came back, he built a house made out of concrete. Each time he built a stronger house. As a child, I didn't realize what my parents were sacrificing. They were working for us to have shelter and a decent place to live, and even then, our family was still broken because my dad was always coming here. At night he waited for us to fall asleep so that he could leave at night so that we couldn't see him leave. And it was a heartbreak over and over again. It got to the point where I sensed that he would be leaving, and I didn't want to go to sleep. I must have been like five years old . . . three years old . . . when these things were happening.

So we spent a lot of our childhood with my mom making tortillas and selling them by the pound to make ends meet. She also had chickens and other creative and resourceful ways of making money. One of the things my mom remembers a lot from our time in Mexico was that while she was working to make tortillas and sell them, my little brother would fall asleep on the walker, the andadera. He would just fall asleep there with a rolled tortilla, a taco, in his hand, while my mom worked, because he couldn't walk. So it was almost like we had a single mom, since my dad was always in the US.

He always sent pictures—posing elegantly. I assume we talked to him on the phone, but I don't remember that. I can't imagine how as a married couple my parents lived through that. All of those years and months and months and months of separation under such difficult circumstances. Financially, and just not having a job and having to sell tortillas and having kids to raise. And so eventually, when I was seven years old, my mom gave my father an ultimatum and said, "We stay here and we starve together, or we go to the US." The plan was to live in US for five years, save money, work a lot, and return home. We needed to be together. So, essentially, that was the moment when my parents were forced to uproot and leave the country where they speak the language and the country that their family lives in to make sure that we would all be together, to make sure that we had better opportunities.

I don't remember the specific moment when my parents told us we were going to the United States. But I remember the conversations that followed where my parents would say little things to get us used to the idea that things would change. They were saying things like . . . when we asked for pesos, they would say, "En los Estados Unidos, no son pesos. Son dólares", which means "in the US, it's not pesos anymore. It's dollars." They were planting the seed to help us transition. I remember not thinking that it would be for life. I didn't think we were going to grow up here, that this would become home. I remember my little brother leaving his bike behind and telling our cousins, to watch his bike for when we returned.

But there were a lot of conversations, and our parents definitely told us we would be undocumented. As a seven-year-old, when someone tells you

you're going to be undocumented, you don't know what that means. So I didn't realize what that status would mean for my life until much later in my tenth grade year of high school. Our status was not hidden from us, but we didn't know what it meant. At the time, we were still in survival mode.

When we arrived, we were safe, and we had people here to welcome us and to make us feel comfortable. My mom started cleaning houses. My dad was working in a Chinese restaurant, and my mom eventually started working in a restaurant as well. We would just go home and someone would watch over us and a bunch of other kids and we would go to bed. Our parents got home after we fell asleep, so we barely saw them. There was no one there to help us with homework because our parents were working hard to get us on our feet and find a place for us to live.

My experience of adapting to this country was much easier than it was for my parents. To this day, they're still trying to learn how to communicate with people, but I learned how to do that in one year and a half. But school was definitely a challenge for us as kids.

I was so jealous of kids who could read and would watch them in anger because I couldn't communicate. I was a great student in Mexico. I knew the content, but I knew it in my language. So being here, those first two years, I just felt so ignorant. I couldn't stand people talking around me because I thought that they were talking about me, which seems silly now, but at the time, I just felt targeted when people spoke English around me. So that jealousy that I had of my classmates who could read in English, pushed me to learn. I came here when I was in the middle of third grade, and by fifth grade, I was in an advanced reading class and was the best student in the class at the end of the year. I learned very quickly.

We grew up walking to school, but in the beginning, we had to ride the bus. The first day riding the bus, I didn't know what bus to get on, so I just got on one of the busses. I assumed it would eventually take me home, and I just stayed on the bus because I never saw the place where we were living. I was the only kid left on the bus, so the bus driver had to bring me back to school. My mom and my aunt were worried and came to pick me up at school. I felt so inadequate.

My little brother had an incident when we first arrived. He was in first grade, and I was in third grade. He didn't know how to ask if he could go use the restroom, so he peed his pants and had to wear the principal's pants for the rest of the day. He was extremely humiliated. Dehumanizing things like that, for a first grader—that just sticks with you forever.

After I learned English, everything was normal. My teachers praised me and always encouraged me and told me that I would do great things and that I would go to college. I did really well in middle school. I think the biggest thing that happened in high school was that my friends started getting driver's licenses, and then I realized that I couldn't obtain one myself. That's when being undocumented started becoming real—I started realizing what it meant.

I had big dreams for a higher education because education has always been something that my parents have emphasized as something that is really important and the key to success and the reason why we're here. The reason that they made that big sacrifice to bring us here. So, I had these huge dreams and aspirations for the colleges that I was going to go to.

When I was a sophomore, in my literature class, we were reading *Night* by Eli Weisel about the Holocaust and his story. I felt really connected to the book, especially after Eli Weisel made the statement that "no human being is illegal." I decided to enter an art contest hosted by the Georgia Commission for the Holocaust. I won third place, and my artwork was going to be on display at a ceremony. I attended with my teacher and my mom. I was going to receive fifty dollars as a prize. So, you know, I was very excited to go. A little bit uncomfortable for my mom because she didn't speak English, and we were the only people of color there from what I remember. I just felt out of place as soon as we walked in. You don't feel like you fit in—especially being at the Capitol building where the ceremony took place. We were in this government building and being undocumented made us feel self-conscious.

We got our awards, and at the end of the ceremony, we were supposed to get our prizes. I remember sitting down and waiting with my mom. My teacher, who was my mentor as well, came back and told me that I couldn't get my prize because I didn't have a social security number. I was confused and angry and didn't know what to say. We just walked away. I didn't say anything, but I had the realization it didn't matter how much work I put into something or how talented I was. Even though someone decided that I deserved it, because I didn't have a set of numbers, because I wasn't born here . . . that would determine a lot of things in my life.

Then I found out that I didn't qualify for federal financial aid. A lot of scholarships are not available to me. I couldn't apply for FAFSA. There are even schools that ban undocumented students. In Georgia, the Board of Regents ban undocumented students from attending the top public universities. On top of that, Georgia's policy is to charge out of state tuition for people who are undocumented.

As I got older and approached my senior year, I realized that doors were just closing on me. My teachers helped me, and I was very open with them about my status. They helped me apply; they helped me contact admissions, and I ended up getting in—I ended up applying to Agnes Scott College through Early Action and that was the light at the end of the tunnel. They had the Goizueta Foundation Scholarship available to undocumented students. The only requirement was that you live in the United States.

I applied for that, wrote the essay, and made it to the next round. I interviewed, and it wasn't until March, right before graduating my senior year, that I found out that I got the scholarship. Every single day after school I had been running down that hill—because I lived down the street from my high school—to the mailbox. I would run down the hill to see if I had gotten any news. So, when I finally got the letter, I ran up the hill and I waited to open it in front of my mom, who was home. I remember we had a pep rally that day so we were all celebrating, the senior class was celebrating because we were all so close to graduation. When I opened that letter I realized . . . just looking at the number and the amount of money I was going to get . . . just mind-blowing. That someone would invest that much money in me to go to school! I felt so humbled.

I went to Agnes Scott. I majored in Studio Art, studied a lot of US History, and learned the true story of this country. I joined Teach for America because my life had been so focused on advocating for undocumented people and undocumented students. At Agnes Scott, I realized that the fight for social justice needs to be fought together and across identities. I wanted to expand that fight into the classroom and to help all of my students. I taught two years at a bilingual elementary school in Clayton County—fifth grade, third and first grades. After I completed my commitment with Teach for America, I transitioned to Dekalb County, which is where I grew up and where I was educated the county's public school system. I came back, and now I'm teaching art at the high school from which I graduated.

I was granted DACA in 2013 between my junior and senior years, of college. When that happened, it was like a window of time where my life would feel normal for that two-year period. There are moments where I think,

"This is so normal. I'm a teacher. I have a job. I can put my degree to use, and I have a driver's license. I can drive without feeling scared." And then, there are moments where that fear, that paralyzing fear, just hits I am reminded of who the president is, and I realize the hate that is driving our immigration policies, and Trump's decision to rescind DACA. I go back between that feeling of being normal and American and that of being terrified . . . maybe not for myself as much, but for my family, for my siblings, for my students.

I was seven years old when we migrated here, and so I didn't necessarily make the decision to give up anything or sacrifice anything. The sacrifice was made by my parents. When I think about what it could have been like if I had stayed where I was when I was growing up, I don't know if I would be as empowered and resilient as I am today. I know that my experience of being undocumented and having to hear "no" all the time has made me this resilient. I'm still very connected to my culture, my language, and my background. I haven't lost that.

It's my parents who lost the ability to see their parents. My mom's dad is here, but I remember when I was in elementary school, soon after we came here, my mom's sister committed suicide. My parents lost the ability to see their family members, who were struggling in Mexico. My dad couldn't see his dad before he passed away because he had cancer. It is so human to be by your loved ones' side when they are passing away or when they're sick. You want to be there and provide support and enjoy last moments with them. My parents didn't get that. It's because of their sacrifice that I must use my voice to speak out.

Ever since Trump was elected, I think it was just a matter of time as to when DACA was going to go away. So DACA was very vulnerable the moment that it became an executive action, and it came about because immigrant youth mobilized and fought to get that to happen. It's time for something better. Our community deserves better. We deserve stability and something more inclusive. DACA has given the nation the opportunity to see us officially. The impact we have been making in our communities is now on paper. This is just a small sample of what we are capable of. Imagine what we will accomplish with a more permanent solution to our broken immigration system.

The American Dream is this idea that is romanticized about what the United States is going to be like. The reality is that there's so much more—things that are happening in this country today are so rooted in the country's history of slavery and racism. So, the American Dream, what I thought it was as a high school student, is completely different now for me. I think that the American Dream is embodied in my parents. My parents' sacrifice, that's the American Dream. It's my students; it's the work that we are doing every day to make sure that they feel safe and protected in their school communities and protecting each other. It's standing up for each other; it's not the beautiful picture of a white picket fence and owning a home. It's not that. It's actually the people that come to this country and make it what it is and have done so for years and years. No one in this country is originally from here, unless they are the indigenous people who this land belongs to. There is always a new population being targeted, and we have to really take a hard look at ourselves as a country and the ignorance of a history that happens over and over again—and will continue happening. We are what makes America great.

I honor my parents' sacrifice, their American Dream by teaching which allows me to serve my community and this country. I will always be an educator and an artist and will always be creating. It's hard to say what's going to happen with me. I don't really know if people who have applied for DACA are going to be targeted by ICE after we lose our work permits, after they start expiring. I'm doing everything that I can between now and until February 2019, which is when my work permit expires, to make sure that my actions are actions of permanency and to paint murals that will be here forever even if I'm not. To touch the lives of my students and plant seeds that will always bloom here. This is what I mean when I say "Here to stay." It's the work that I do with my students every day and through my artwork. So regardless of what happens to me physically, whether I'm deported or not, so much of me will still be here.

VIDEO LINKS

greencardvoices.org/speakers/yehimi-cambrón

Afterword

Learning from the students' stories in this book is just the beginning. The more important work starts when we engage in difficult but necessary conversations about the changing face of our nation.

Immigration plays a significant role in modern America; one in five Americans speak a language other than English at home. From classrooms to bookclubs, from the individual interested in learning more about his immigrant neighbor to the business owner looking to understand her employees and business partners, this book is an important resource for all Americans.

For these reasons, we have included a portion of our Act4Change study guide, a glossary, and links to the students' video narratives, intended to expand the impact of these students' journeys to the United States. The Act4Change study guide is an experiential learning tool. It promotes participation scaffolded with thoughtful discussion questions and activities that are designed for hands-on learning, emphasizing personal growth. It will help teachers, students, and all participants examine their own stories.

We hope to spark deeply meaningful conversations about identity, appreciation of difference, and our shared human experience.

If you would like to learn more about speaking events, traveling exhibits, and other ways to engage with the *Green Card Youth Voices* stories, visit our website—www.greencardvoices.org.

Act4Change:
A Green Card Voices Study Guide

Each person has the power to tell their own story in their own voice. The art of storytelling translates across cultures and over time. In order to learn about and appreciate voices other than our own, we must be exposed to and given tools to foster an understanding of a variety of voices. We must be able to view the world from others' perspectives in order to act as agents of change in today's world.

Green Card Youth Voices is comprised of the inspirational voices from a young group of recent immigrants to the US that can be shared with a wide audience. This study guide will provide readers with questions to help them explore universal themes, such as storytelling, immigration, identity, and perspective.

Introduce New Voices:

Participants will select one of the twenty-one storytellers featured in *Green Card Youth Voices* and adopt that person's story as his or her own "new voice." For example, one participant may choose Farhat Sadat while another might choose Mario. Participants will become familiar with the life story of their "new voice" and develop a personal connection to it. After each participant has chosen his or her "new voice," read the personal essay first and then watch the video.

Act4Change 1 :

Answer the following questions—

1. Why did you select the storyteller that you did?
2. What was interesting to you about his/her story?
3. What do you and the storyteller have in common?
4. What have you learned as a result of reading/listening to this person's story?

Learn About New Voices 1:

Divide participants into groups of three or four people. Provide each group with copies of the written narratives from five selected stories. Each person within each group will read one of the five narratives. Once finished, the participants will share their narratives with the others. Then, as a group, choose one of the five "voices" and watch that person's video.

Afterward, go on to the journal activity below.

Act4Change 2:

Answer the following questions—

1. What new information about immigrants did you learn from this second storyteller?
2. Compare and contrast the storyteller's video to his/her story. Which did you prefer? Why?
3. What are some similarities between you and the second storyteller?
4. If this really was your "new voice," what might you want to know about America upon arriving?
5. If you could only bring one suitcase on your move to another country, what would you pack in it? Why?

Learn About New Voices 2:

Each participant will be given a third "new voice," and only one can go to each student; there can be no duplicates.

Inform participants not to share the identity of their "new voice." Participants will try to match their classmates' "new voices" to one of the stories in the book. Encourage participants to familiarize themselves with all of the voices featured in *Green Card Youth Voices*.

Act4Change 3:

1. After they are given their "new voice," ask participants to try and create connections between this third voice and themselves. Have the students read their story and then watch the video of their "new voice." Have them think of a piece of art, dance, song, spokenword, comic, sculpture, or other medium of their choosing that best describes their "new voice."

2. Participants will present a 3-5 minute artistic expression for the larger group from the perspective of their "new voice" in thirty-five minutes. The audience will have a template with a chart that includes each of the thirty GCYV students' names, their photo, and a one- or two-sentence abbreviated biography. Audience members will use this chart throughout the activities to keep track of what has been learned about each voice that they have heard.

3. Ask the participants to describe the relationship between the Green Card Youth Voices and themselves:

    a. What did you notice about the form of artistic expression and the story?

    b. What drew you to this specific art form?

    c. Do you notice any cultural relationships between the "new voice" and the piece of art that was chosen?

    d. What is your best advice to immigrant students on how to succeed in this country? State? City?

More than Meets the Eye:

In small groups, have participants read and watch three or four selected narratives from *Green Card Youth Voices*. After that, have group members tell each other facts about themselves and tell the others in the group what they would not know just by looking at them. For example, participants can share an interesting talent, a unique piece of family history, or a special interest. Then have group members discuss things that they found surprising about the students in *Green Card Youth Voices*.

Think about the "new voice" you transformed in Act4Change 3. Tell your group something that was "more than meets the eye" from the perspective of that "new voice!"

For the complete version of Act4Change: A Green Card Voices Study Guide, visit our website—www.greencardvoices.org

See also:

Act4Change: A Green Card Youth Voices Study Guide, Workshop for Educators
This workshop is a focused learning experience crafted to deepen teacher understanding and provide instructional strategy, particularly designed to be used in conjunction with *Green Card Youth Voices*.

Glossary

Accountant: a person whose job is to keep or inspect financial accounts

Advance Parole: a permit for a non-citizen, who does not have a valid immigrant visa, to re-enter the United States after traveling abroad

Akon: an American singer, songwriter, businessman, record producer, and actor of Senegalese descent

American Dream: the ideal that every US citizen should have an equal opportunity to achieve success and prosperity through hard work, determination, and initiative

American Refugee Committee (ARC): an international nonprofit, nonsectarian organization that works with its partners and constituencies to provide opportunities and expertise to communities of refugees and internally displaced persons

Amharic: the official working language of Ethiopia

Anime: a style of hand-drawn and computer animation originating in, and commonly associated with, Japan

Arabic: a central Semitic language that first emerged in Iron Age northwestern Arabia and is now the common language of the Arab world

Baja California: a Mexican state on the Baja California Peninsula, bordering the US state of California

Básico: the Spanish world for "basic"; when used in the phrase "escuela básica" it is taken to mean elementary school

Beta Club: an organization for 4th through 12th graders with a purpose of "promoting the ideals of academic achievement, character, leadership and service among elementary and secondary school students"

Burma: a sovereign state in southeast Asia, now known as Myanmar

Burmese: a citizen of Burma; also the official language of Myanmar

Case Manager: a person who assesses, plans, facilitates, coordinates care, evaluates, and advocates options and services to meet an individual's and family's needs through communication and available resources to promote quality, cost-effective outcomes

Chin State: a state in western Myanmar

Civil Engineer: an engineer that designs and maintains roads, bridges, dams, and similar structures

Culture Shock: a feeling of disorientation experienced by someone who suddenly subjected to an unfamiliar culture, way of life, or set of attitudes

Dakar: the largest and capital city of Senegal in West Africa

Deferred Action for Childhood Arrivals (DACA): an American immigration policy that allowed some individuals who entered the country as minors, and had either entered or remained in the country illegally, to receive a renewable two-year period of deferred action from deportation and to be eligible for a work permit

DeKalb: the fourth-most populous county in Georgia; located east of the City of Atlanta; considered the most diverse county in Georgia

Desiigner: an American rapper, singer, songwriter, record producer, record executive, and actor

Dhaka, Bangladesh: the largest and capital city of Bangladesh

Diversity Visa (D.V.): also known as "green card lottery," a United States government program for receiving a United States Permanent Resident Card

Dólares: the Spanish word for "dollar"

DREAM (Development, Relief, and Education for Alien Minors) Act: an American legislative proposal for a multi-phase process for qualifying undocumented minors in the United States that would first grant conditional residency and, upon meeting further qualifications, permanent residency

Dubai, United Arab Emirates (UAE): the largest and most populous city in the UAE located on the southeast coast of the Persian Gulf

Early Action: term used when applying to college; different from Early Decision, Early Action plans are non-binding and allow an applicant to receive an early response but do not have to commit until the normal reply date

El Rio: translates from Spanish into "The River"

Embassy: the official residence or offices of an ambassador in another country

English to Speakers of Other Languages (ESOL): the use or study of English by speakers of other languages

Es: the Spanish world for "is"

Escuintla, Guatemala: a city in south central Guatemala

Eso: the Spanish word for "that"

Fantasy: a genre of fiction, which typically depicts original worlds and characters imbued supernatural or magical elements.

Farmers Market: a food market at which local farmers sell fruit and vegetables —and often meat, cheese, and bakery products—directly to consumers

Forest Park: a city in Clayton County, Georgia approximately nine miles south of Atlanta

Future: an American rapper, singer, songwriter, and record producer

Gambia: a country in West Africa that is primarily surrounded by Senegal except the Atlantic Ocean on its western side

Gato: the Spanish word for "cat"

Goizueta Foundation: established by Roberto C. Goizueta in 1992, the foundation provides assistance to educational and charitable institutions

Guinea: a country in West Africa, bordered on the west by the Atlantic Ocean

Halal: denoting or relating to meat prepared as prescribed by Muslim law

Hartsfield-Jackson International Airport: The name of the Atlanta airport, which is the busiest airport in the world.

Hillsong: an Australian Christian music praise and worship group from Sydney, Australia, that formed in 1983

Huehuetenango, Guatemala: a city and municipality in the highlands of western Guatemala; capital of the Department of Huehuetenango

Immigration and Customs Enforcement: a US federal government law enforcement agency under the jurisdiction of the Department of Homeland Security with two primary concepts: Homeland Security Investigations and Enforcement & Removal Operations

International Center: the DeKalb International Student Center

International Organization for Migration (IOM): an intergovernmental organization that provides services and advice concerning migration to governments and migrants, including internally displaced persons, refugees, and migrant workers

Istanbul: the most populous city in Turkey and the country's cultural, economic, and historic center; is transcontinental with half of the country in Europe and half in Asia, and is historically known as Constantinople and Byzantium

Kabuli Palaw: also known as Qabli, it is a northern Afghan dish made from a variety of pilaf consisting of steamed rice mixed with raisins, carrots, and lamb

Kalaymyo, Myanmar: a town in the Sagaing Division of Myanmar

Kigali: the capitol and largest city in Rwanda

Lamina: a thin, layered substance, which can be made from a variety of materials

Maize: corn

Malaysia: a federal constitutional monarchy consisting of thirteen states and three federal territories located in southeast Asia

Mali: a landlocked country in West Africa that is regionally identified with the West African Craton

Mango: a juicy stone fruit from numerous species of tropical trees

Mechanical Engineer: applies engineering, physics, and materials science principles to design, analyze, manufacture, and maintain mechanical systems

Milo: a chocolate and malt powder that is mixed with hot or cold water or milk to produce a beverage popular mainly in Australia, New Zealand, Malaysia, Thailand, South Africa, and other parts of the world

Mojados: a highly derogatory term for one who crosses an international border by passing through a body of water by wading, swimming, etc. from the shore of one country to illegally enter the adjacent country

Myanmar: a southeast Asian nation, formerly known as Burma, consisting of more than 100 ethnic groups that borders India, Bangladesh, China, Laos, and Thailand

Myanmar vs. Burma: both names relate to the southeast Asian nation and can be used interchangeably; in 1989, the ruling military government changed the name from Burma to Myanmar officially after an uprising killed thousands

Oromo: an ethnic group inhabiting Ethiopia and parts of Kenya and Somalia

Paris: France's capital, and a major European city and a global center for art, fashion, gastronomy, and culture

Pesos: the basic monetary unit of Mexico

Persian: an Iranian ethnic group that make up over half of the population of Iran; also known as Farsi, one of the Western Iranian languages within the Indo-Iranian branch of the Indo-European language family

Phobia: an extreme or irrational fear of or aversion to something

Porter: a person employed to carry luggage and other loads

Properties: refers to owned land or developments (houses, stores, restaurants, etc.)

Questbridge: a non-profit program that links students with educational and scholarship opportunities at some US colleges and universities

Ramadan: the ninth month of the Islamic calendar. The holiday is observed by fasting for the month in order to celebrate the revelation of the Quran to Muhammad

Rajshahi, Bangladesh: a metropolitan city and major urban, commercial, and educational centre of North Bengal

Refugee Camp: a temporary settlement built to receive refugees and people in refugee-like situations that usually accommodate people who have fled their home countries

Refugee School: schools constructed and set up in refugee camps for the children within the camps

Rickshaw: a light, two-wheeled hooded vehicle drawn by one or more people

Sai Sai: a well-known Burmese singer-songwriter, model, novelist, and actor of ethnic Shan descent

Senegal: a country on Africa's west coast with a rich French colonial heritage and many natural attractions

STEM: Science, Technology, Engineering, and Math

"Special School": refers to a remedial English courses taken by the student.

Stanford: a private research university in Stanford, California, located 20 miles outside of San Jose

Sylhet, Bangladesh: a metropolitan city in northeastern Bangladesh, also known as Jalalabad, the spiritual capital. People from there are called Sylhetis

Tabaski: the Senegal word for "Feast of the Sacrifice"; a muslim holiday celebrated worldwide each year to honor the willingness of Ibrahim (Abraham) to sacrifice his son, as an act of obedience to God's command

Taka: the currency of the People's Republic of Bangladesh

Takis: a roll-shaped snack fashioned after the traditional Mexican taquito

Taliban: refers to itself as the Islamic Emirate of Afghanistan (IEA) and has been described as a movement of religious students from the Pashtun areas of eastern and southern Afghanistan who had been educated in traditional Islamic schools in Pakistan, and as a Sunni Islamic fundamentalist political movement in Afghanistan currently waging war within that country

Tambacounda: the largest city in eastern Senegal, 400 kilometres from Dakar, and is the regional capital of the province of the same name

Teach for America (TFA): a nonprofit organization that recruits and selects college graduates from top universities from around the United States to serve as teachers

Tijuana, Mexico: the largest city in the Mexican state of Baja California

Tlangpi: a Myanmar Chin state

Tuberculosis (TB): an infectious bacterial disease that mainly affects the lungs

Un: the Spanish word for "a"

United Nations (U.N.): an intergovernmental organization tasked to promote international cooperation and to create and maintain international order

Visa: an official government document that temporarily authorizes you to be in the country you are visiting

Wolof: a language of Senegal, the Gambia and Mauritania, and the native language of the Wolof people

About the Advisory Team

Tea Rozman Clark, PhD is the Executive Director of Green Card Voices. She is an NYU graduate in Near and Middle Eastern studies and has a PhD in Cultural History, specializing in oral history recording from the University of Nova Gorica. She is first generation immigrant from Slovenia and 2015 Bush Leadership Fellow.

Rachel Mueller is the Program Manager at Green Card Voices. She is a graduate of Macalester College where she studied Anthropology and African Studies. She attended Waterford Kamhlaba United World College of Southern Africa in Swaziland where she lived for two years.

José Guzmán is the Lead Graphic Designer and Video Editor at Green Card Voices. He graduated from St. Olaf College in 2014 where he earned a BA in Studio Art.

Zamzam Ahmed is the Program Associate at Green Card Voices. She graduated from St. Catherine University with a degree in Political Science and International Relations.

Darlene Xiomara Rodriguez, PhD, MSW, MPA is an Assistant Professor of Social Work and Human Services at Kennesaw State University. She is a Diversity Fellow with the Center for Diversity Leadership and Engagement. Her teaching, research, and public service are focused on civic engagement, immigrant integration, and nonprofit management.

Lara Smith-Sitton, PhD is the Director of Community Engagement and Assistant Professor of English at Kennesaw State University. Her teaching and research areas include community engagement, professional writing, and 18th- and 19th-Century rhetoric.

Yehimi Cambrón is an immigrant artist based in Atlanta, GA and an art teacher at Cross Keys High School. She graduated from Agnes Scott with a BA in Studio Art and her artwork focuses on celebrating the resiliency and humanity of immigrants.

About Green Card Voices

Founded in 2013, Green Card Voices (GCV) is a nonprofit organization that utilizes storytelling to share personal narratives of America's immigrants, establishing a better understanding between the immigrant and nonimmigrant population. Our dynamic, video-based platform, book collections, and traveling exhibits are designed to empower a variety of educational institutions, community groups, and individuals to acquire first-person perspectives about immigrants' lives, increasing the appreciation of the immigrant experience in America.

Green Card Voices was born from the idea that the broad narrative of current immigrants should be communicated in a way that is true to each immigrant's story. We seek to be a new lens for those in the immigration dialogue and build a bridge between immigrants and nonimmigrants—newcomers and the receiving community—from across the country. We do this by sharing the firsthand immigration stories of foreign-born Americans, by helping others to see the "wave of immigrants" as individuals, with interesting stories of family, hard work, and cultural diversity.

To date, the Green Card Voices team has recorded the life stories of over three hundred immigrants coming from more than one hundred different countries. All immigrants that decide to share their story with GCV are asked six open-ended questions. In addition, they are asked to share personal photos of their life in their country of birth and in the US. The video narratives are edited down to five-minute videos filled with personal photographs, an intro, an outro, captions, and background music. These video stories are available on www.greencardvoices.org, and YouTube (free of charge and advertising).

Green Card Youth Voices: Immigration Stories from an Atlanta High School is the fourth in a series of many books that GCV hopes to publish in other cities as well; future series that we are working on include: *Green Card Entrepreneur Voices* and *Green Card Artist Voices*.

Contact information:
Green Card Voices
2854 Columbus Ave South
Minneapolis, MN 55407

www.greencardvoices.org
612.889.7635

Facebook: www.facebook.com/GreenCardVoices
Twitter: www.twitter.com/GreenCardVoices

Immigrant Youth Traveling Exhibits

Twenty students' stories from each city in the *Green Card Youth Series* (Atlanta, Minneapolis, Fargo, and St. Paul) are featured in traveling exhibits, available to schools, universities, libraries, and other venues where communities gather. Each exhibit features twenty stories from a particular city, each with a portrait, a 200-word biography, and a quote from each immigrant. A QR code is displayed next to each portrait and can be scanned with a mobile device to watch the digital stories. The following programming can be provided with the exhibit: panel discussions, presentations, and community-building events.

Green Card Voices currently has seven exhibits based on different communities across the Midwest and South. To rent an exhibit, please contact us at 612.889.7635 or info@greencardvoices.com.

Green Card Youth Voices: Book Readings

Meeting the student authors in person creates a dynamic space in which to engage with these topics firsthand. Book readings are a wonderful opportunity to hear the students share their stories and answer questions about their lived experiences.

To schedule a book reading in your area, please contact us at 612.889.7635 or info@greencardvoices.com.

Now available:

Green Card Youth Voices:

Immigration Stories from a Minneapolis High School

The first book in the Green Card Youth Voices series, *Green Card Youth Voices: Immigration Stories from a Minneapolis High School* is a unique book of personal essays written by students from Wellstone International High School. Coming from 13 different countries, these young people share stories of family, school, change, and dreams. The broad range of experiences and the honesty with which these young people tell their stories is captured here with inspiring clarity. Available as an ebook (ISBN: 978-0-9974960-1-7) and paperback (ISBN : 978-0-9974960-0-0).

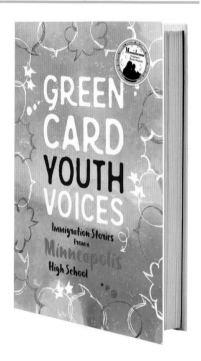

Contents:

- Full color portraits
- 30 personal essays by students from around the world
- Links to digital video stories on the Green Card Voices website
- Foreword by Kao Kalia Yang, award-winning author of *The Latehomecomer* and *The Song Poet*
- Excerpt from *Act4Change: A Green Card Voices Study Guide*
- Glossary

2016 Moonbeam Children's Gold Medal for Multicultural Non-Fiction Chapter Book   Foreword INDIES Finalist for Young Adult Nonfiction   Independent Press Awards winner for Best Young Adult Nonfiction

> To purchase online and view a list of retailers, visit greencardvoices.org/books.
>
> Also available on Amazon.

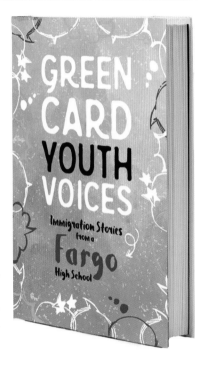

Also available:
Green Card Youth Voices:
Immigration Stories from a St. Paul High School

Based on the successful model used in Minneapolis, MN and Fargo, ND, *Green Card Youth Voices: Immigration Stories from a St. Paul High School* features 30 student authors from LEAP High School and is a vehicle to generate awareness about the immigrant experience. The book includes links to the students' video narrative, a study guide, and glossary to help teachers use the book as an educational resource when teaching about immigration. Available as an ebook (ISBN: 978-0-9974960-5-5) and paperback (ISBN : 978-0-9974960-3-1).

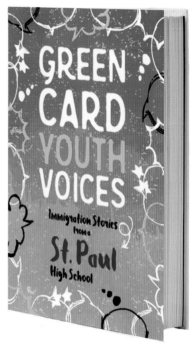

Midwest Book Awards Finalist
for Young Adult Nonfiction

Contents:

- Full color portraits
- 30 personal essays by students from around the world
- Links to digital video stories on the Green Card Voices website
- Excerpt from *Act4Change: A Green Card Voices Study Guide*
- Glossary

> To purchase online and view a list of retailers,
> visit greencardvoices.org/books.
>
> Also available on Amazon.

Voices of Immigrant Storytellers:
Teaching Guide for Middle and High Schools

This 10-lesson curriculum based on the Common Core standards was written and designed by immigrants. The teaching guide progressively unfolds the humanity, diversity, and contributions of new American citizens and siutates students' own stories alongside these narratives using eleven Green Card Voices' video narratives. This teaching guide is adaptable for grades 6-12. Available as an ebook (ISBN: 978-0-692-51151-0) and paperback (ISBN: 978-0-692-57281-8).

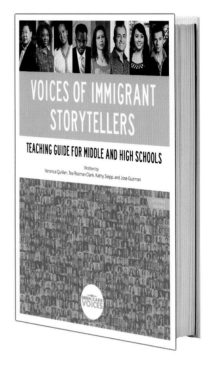

Includes:
- 72 illustrated pages
- 11 Green Card Voices Stories
- 7 ready-to-use worksheets
- 8 classroom activities
- 2 field trip suggestions
- 20 online resources

Available at
greencardvoices.org/books
teacherspayteachers.com
amazon.com

For more information, visit our website at www.greencardvoices.org
or contact us at info@greencardvoices.com